# POWER CARVING HOUSE SPIRITS WITH TOM WOLFE

Text written with and photography by Jeffrey B. Snyder

Schiffer Publishing Ltd

77 Lower Valley Road, Atglen, PA 19310

Printed in China

ISBN: 0-7643-0183-7

Library of Congress Cataloging-in-Publication Data

Wolfe, Tom (Tom James)
    Power carving house spirits with Tom Wolfe/
text written with and photography by Jeffrey B.
Snyder.
      p.     cm.
    ISBN 0-7643-0183-7
    1. Wood-carving.  2. Power tools.  3. Spirits in
art.  I. Snyder, Jeffrey B.  II. Title.
TT199.7.W6428   1997
736'.4--dc20                              96-9896
                                            CIP

Published by Schiffer Publishing Ltd.
77 Lower Valley Road
Atglen, PA 19310
Phone: (610) 593-1777
Fax: (610) 593-2002
Please write for a free catalog.
This book may be purchased from the publisher.
Please include $2.95 for shipping.
Try your bookstore first.

We are interested in hearing from authors
with book ideas on related subjects.

# Contents

# Acknowledgments

I would like to thank the following suppliers for their help: Smoky Mountain Woodcarvers Supply, Inc., P.O. Box 82, Townsend, TN 37882 and Woodcraft Supply Corp., P.O. Box 1686, Parkersburg, WV  26102-1686

# Introduction

I think house spirits are closely related to wood spirits, powerful creatures who keep watch over the woodlands. I first began carving wood spirits in the late 1960s. I got the idea for those wood spirits when I was in England. I was talking with Gail Haley, a well known author of children's books, while riding out to meet Willard Watson, a widely respected mountain toy maker and friend. Gail collects old-time toys. While riding along, I asked her to write me a short story to put on a hang tag for my walking sticks. Now Gail had written a book called *The Green Man, the English Wild Man.* She asked me what I called my man, and I told her I had been calling him a wood spirit. She wrote the story I later put in the book *Wood Spirits and Walking Sticks.*

Perhaps the house spirits found here are transplanted wood spirits straight from their beloved forests, carried unnoticed in the cut timbers and milled wood found throughout any home. In England you find house spirits in the obvious and sometimes in the least obvious places, peeping out of a nook, niche, or cubby hole. They are found up high, down low, on barn rafters, in houses and outhouses (WC's as the English call them). They also frequent the Green Man's Pub ... I only know this because I have been there for the food mind you, I'd never touch a drop! That could be why some were carved from stone ... a stoned green man. The ones I saw cut from stone were carved to look like wood.

Whatever material was used, the house spirit always had that all-knowing smile, or smirk, stern but friendly. They are always apart, always alone, but always close by.

In any case, house spirits are strong, capable of taming the wildest house pet or driving off tiresome guests or relatives who have overstayed their welcome. Still, their strength is tempered with gentleness. They are kind to children, maidens, and good hearted men.

Any home inhabited by a house spirit will stand protected for many years. Families who give their house spirit an honored place in the home, treat it with kindness, give it a name, and include it in conversations and jokes will be blessed with the best of luck, happiness and good health.

With a keen eye, house spirits can be found almost anywhere. House spirits are carved from anything that comes out of or goes into a house. These items can be piano legs, wooden braces, exposed timbers, things like that. I carved several of my house spirits into hand hewn wooden timbers recovered from a very old home in the mountains. The house spirits watched over this old homestead for many, many years. I feel house spirits are my friends, I see them in every piece of wood. You will too if you look.

# Tools and Patterns

This house spirit project was carved with power tools. Equipment needed to complete the project includes a bandsaw to cut out the blank, a power reciprocating chisel (I use one by Ryobi although the Automac is also a fine machine and I have used it many times) with spring steel chisel blades called Flexcut Carving Tools, a High Tech hand tool (a dental tool) and a flexible shaft Foredom — both fitted with a series of ruby and diamond cutting and grinding burrs in a variety of shapes, a router, a drill, and a small 7/32" eye punch. For small detail work, sometimes only a pocket knife will do. I prefer a Case pocket knife. The completed project will be sanded with 300 (or 320) and 400 grit sandpaper. It will be finished using Briwax Golden Oak Stain. Enjoy your house spirit!

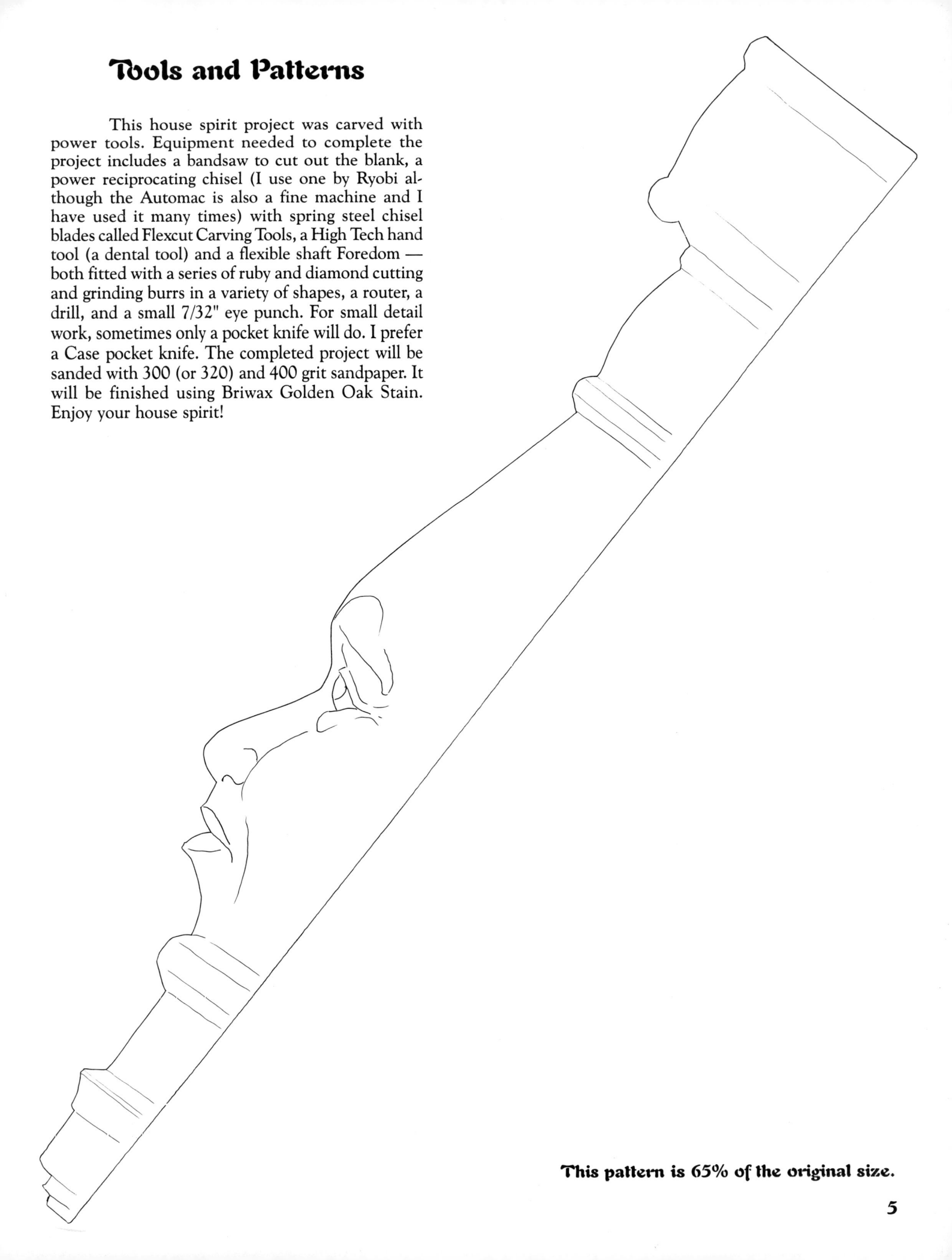

**This pattern is 65% of the original size.**

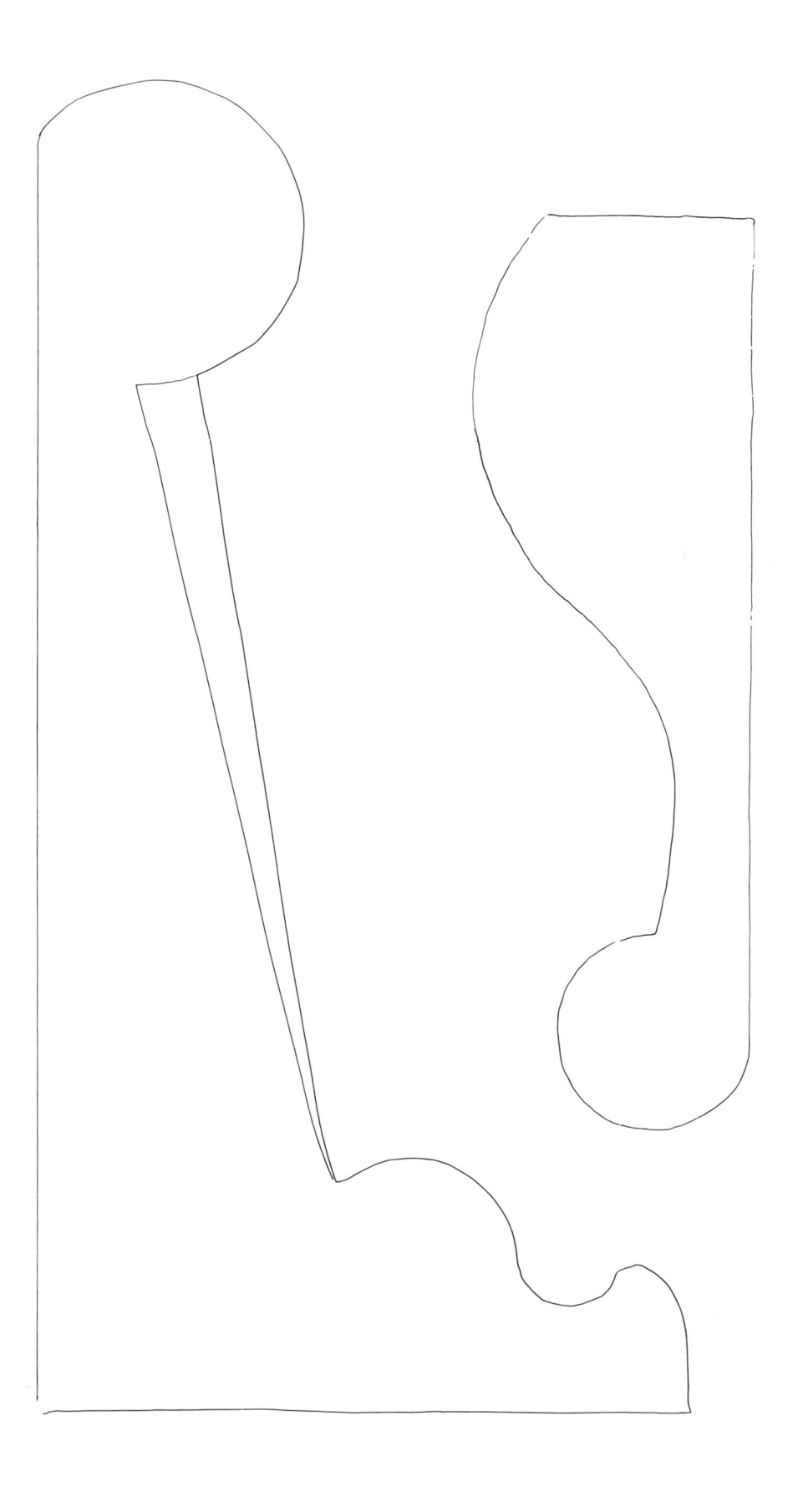

These patterns are 50% of the original size.

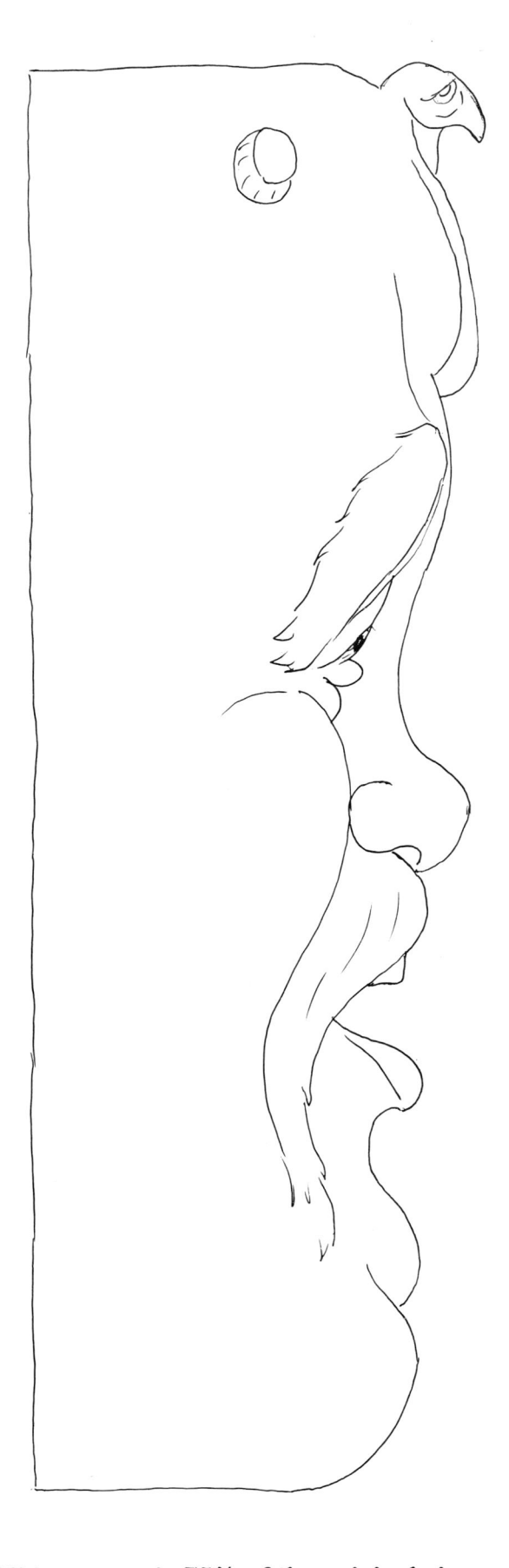

**This pattern is 75% of the original size.**

**This pattern is the original size.**

8

# Carving the House Spirit

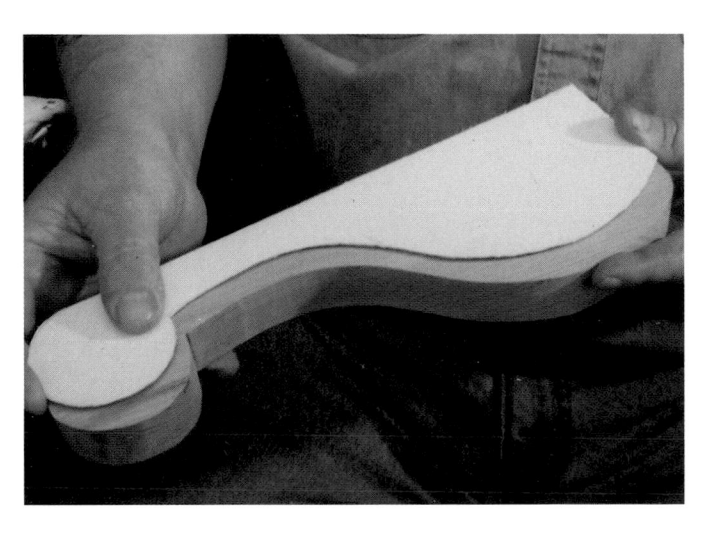

This house spirit will be carved from butternut. Butternut is probably my favorite wood to carve. It is getting expensive and hard to find but it is worth the price. This particular piece, measuring a full inch thick, will go on either side of the head. We will carve it later, following this pattern. You can get this wood in exactly the thickness you need by looking in the Yellow Pages and calling a Dimension Hardwood Mill. They can either get you wood or piece it together to any thickness. The bottom line is that you can fit the piece to any size you choose. It does not have to be this size.

This is 1 1/2" thick butternut walnut. It is 1 1/2" thick because that is what I could get at the time. I used a hand router to create a double router cut along the edge, although any nice router cut will do. The same effect can be made by adding molding to the edge of the board and other things like that. This is the bottom piece.

These are three pieces with similar edge treatments that I have laminated together to make the top piece.

This is a hand held power reciprocating chisel by Ryobi. The blades are sold by Smoky Mountain Woodcarvers Supply and are made of spring steel. They work very well with this product. I am using a half round (or #9) blade for the following cuts.

Like this.

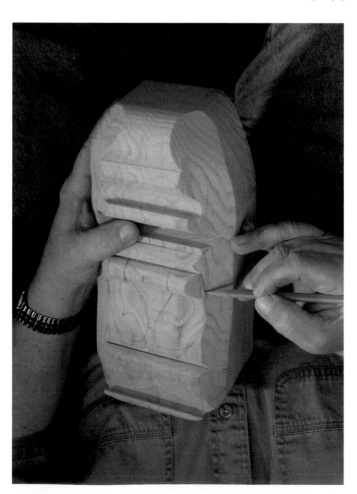

This is the center mark on the carving. Find this to keep everything in balance. I am going to make some basic marks on the piece where I want things like eye sockets. Not only did I saw out the silhouette on the bandsaw but I also used the bandsaw to take off some of the excess wood. I knew I wood was coming off as well.

This is going to be the house spirit's face. House spirits are like wood spirits or gargoyles. They can be carved on anything you are going to put in the house.

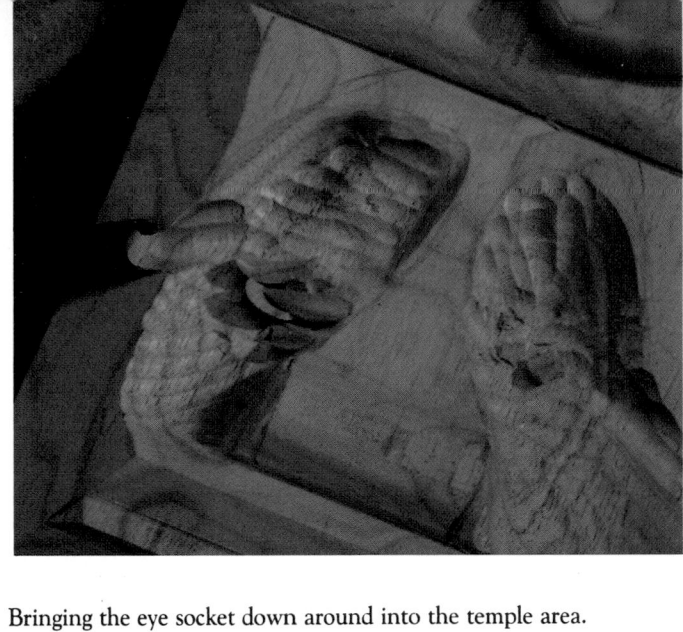

I like to start working around the eyes and nose. Leave the nose good and wide. You can always cut more off but you can never put it back on.

Bringing the eye socket down around into the temple area.

I'm cutting into the eye socket. Leave the bridge of the nose in place.

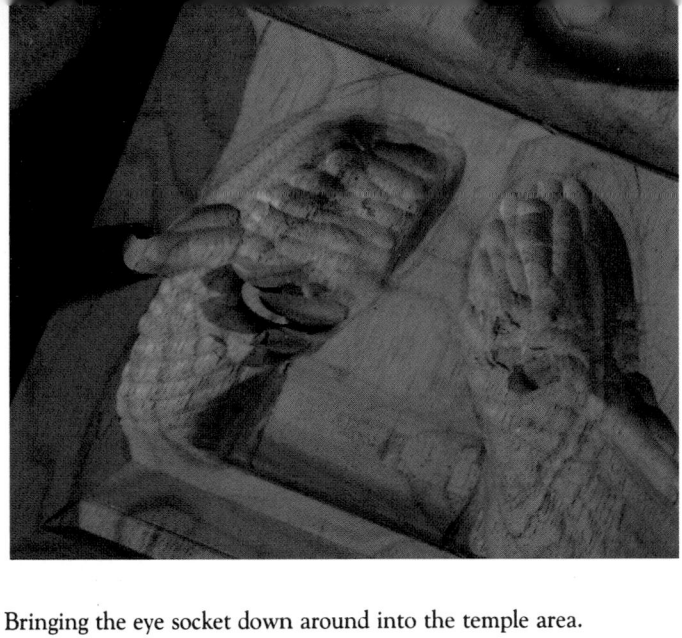

Right now I'm working on down past the nose to create its silhouette. This chisel cuts across the grain better than any other way. I am not working on the eyes or cheeks yet as I'm not working deep enough yet to worry about them.

The eye sockets are now cut into the temple area. Note how this cut is starting to bring the cheek out.

Follow around to the lower lip when roughing out the smile line. Also take a close look at where I place my thumb, both to use pressure points and to keep it out of the way.

This is a inexpensive ball shaped burr you can get at any hardware store. Attached to a flexible shaft Foredom power tool, it roughs out pretty well. It leaves a lot of "wooly-nasties" but they will come out later. I am using the ball shaped burr to put in the smile line on the opposite side to show that it can be carved either way.

Cutting in the smile line. Leave enough material for a mustache. You might want to add one later. Keep your mind open to possibilities and you may come out with a piece that is better than the one you had in mind when you started.

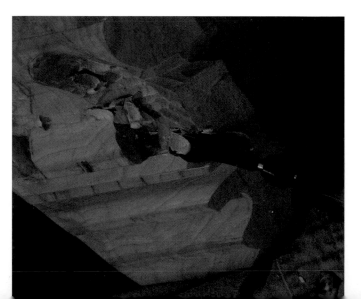

Working to get both eye sockets even. Many times if you turn the piece upside down you will see things more clearly from a different perspective.

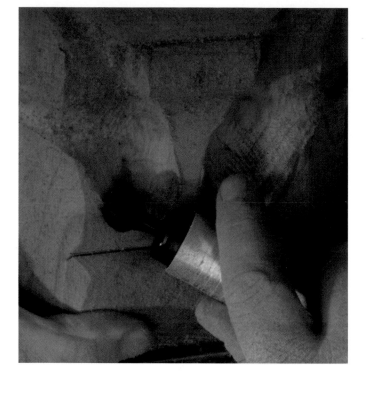

Cleaning up and increasing the depth around the eyes.

This is a High Tech hand tool from Smoky Mountain Woodcarvers Supply. It is made for dentists with two interchangeable heads so you can use two different sized burrs. This is a good, high torque machine. I am also using a cylindrical Kutzall burr.

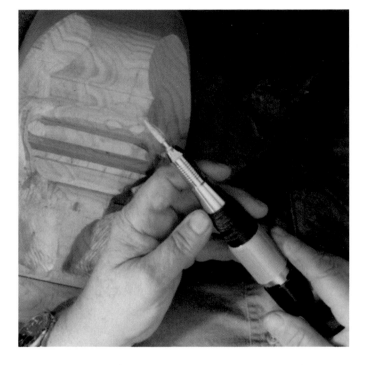

Using a V shaped blade, place a shallow V along the side of the nose and down the smile line to add depth and shape.

Roughing out the excess wood around the teeth (in the areas I blacked out previously) with the High Tech. Round down the outer edges of the teeth as well.

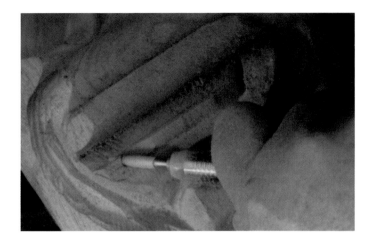

I have decided to include a mustache. I will need to cut down the teeth until they appear to be showing beneath the mustache. Here I am blacking out the mouth around the teeth.

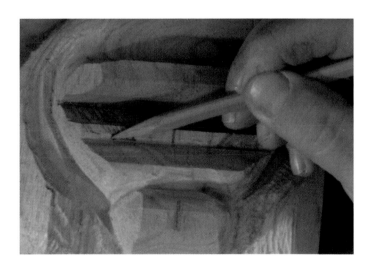

Knock off the corners of the nose to give a place for the nostril. You can used the cylindrical burr almost like a knife when removing material.

Now I have a real plain lower edge line to the lip as you can see here. I can go back and round down around the lip now.

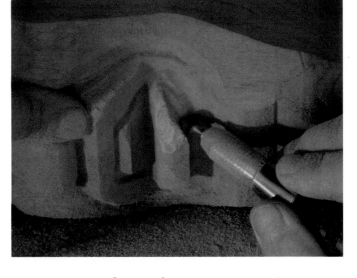

I need to round over the lower lip now before I finish rounding down the outer edges. The unrounded shape would give me false ideas.

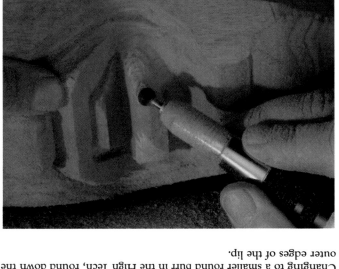

Changing to a smaller round burr in the High Tech, round down the outer edges of the lip.

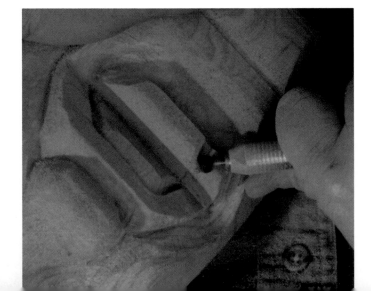

Now we have to cut down the lower lip, sizing it to match the upper lip.

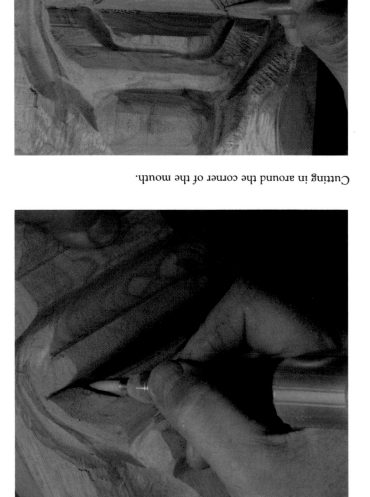

Cutting in around the corner of the mouth.

I have put in a shallow seam line down the middle of the lower lip. People with full lips often have this line. Here is a look at the overall face so far.

Work in under the upper teeth as well to give you nice shadow lines. Shadow lines work for you and can represent many things. Make sure to take full advantage of shadow lines in your work.

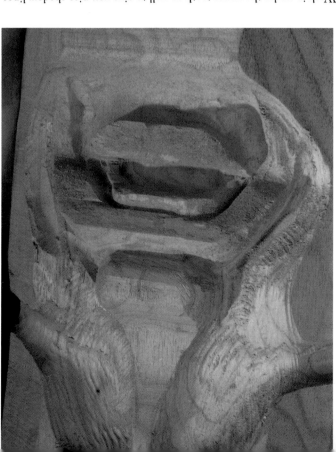

You can extend these burrs in the High Tech quite a ways along their shafts before they become wobbly. Extend the ball shaped burr and hollow out inside the lower lip area. This will create shadows that we want in the mouth.

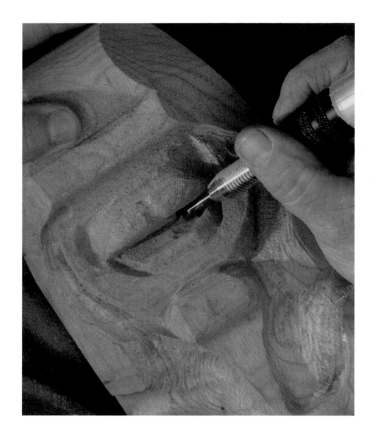

While I have the round burr in place, I'll work around the nose and size it up a bit. Start by cutting in the nostrils. They don't go exactly where they really should so that you can get in the ball of the nose. If you put them in the right place they wouldn't look right.

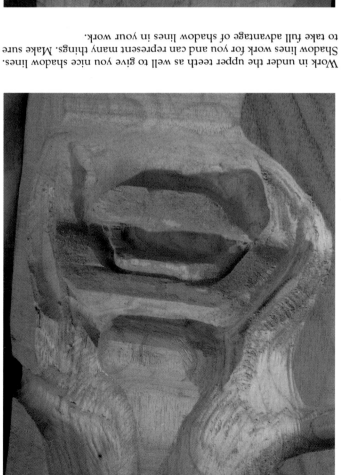

Round off the flanges up into the ball of the nose and on up the side of the nose a bit toward the bridge. The rounded flanges and nostrils are now in place.

Using this heavy handle and a ball shaped burr on the flexible shaft Foredom, round down the roughed out forehead around the hair. If you work it just right, you can leave hair lines as you go using this ball shaped burr. But watch out, the Foredom will overcut very quickly.

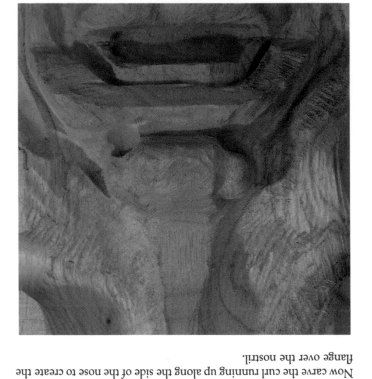

The hair is roughed out.

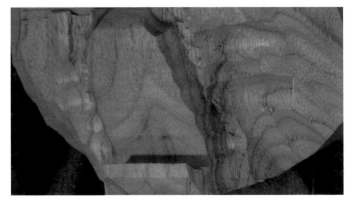

Now carve the curl running up along the side of the nose to create the flange over the nostril.

Switching back to the chisel (although this step can be done with either the rotary tool or the chisel), I'm going to move up to the hair and work it up into the top crest at the upper edge of the piece to make it look like the hair curls over at the top of the forehead. Use a little flatter shaped chisel than the half round I used before. Round-ing down the excess wood on either side of the hair.

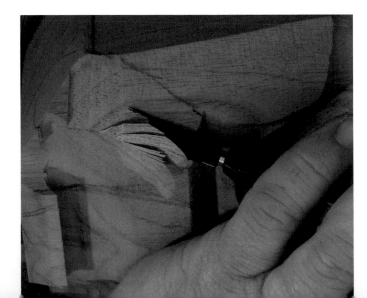

You can also use this burr to shape in the eyebrow as you go.

The shaped forehead and horns.

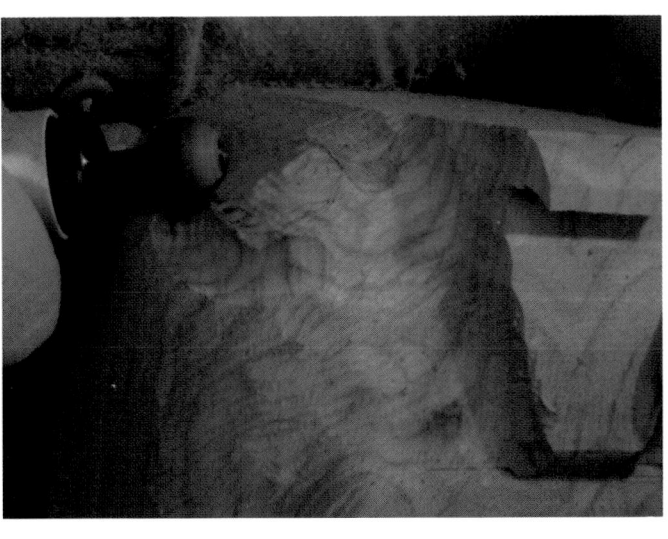

So many people think horns are demonic but that is not the case until later days (the past 60 to 100 years). Always before horns were a sign of strength. Michael Angelo's Moses has horns. Draw in little button shaped horns here if you like. They will balance out the head well.

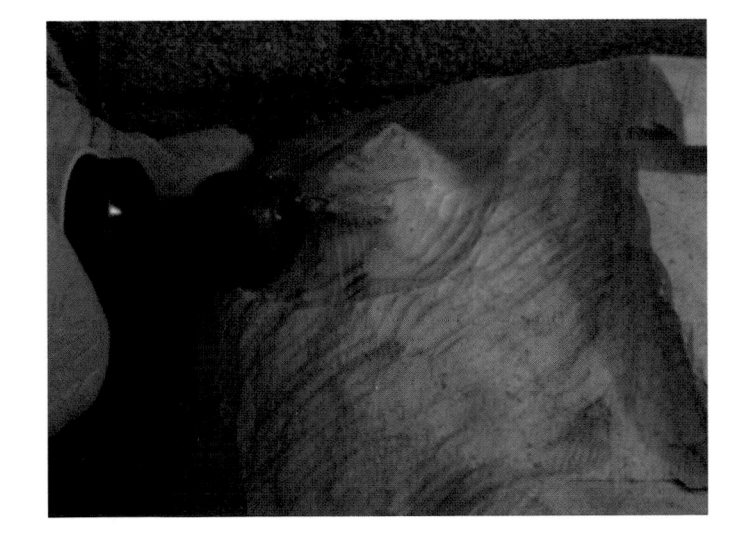

Shaping the horns.

Round down, clean up, and refine the details at this point using the ball shaped burr in the Foredom. Like this.

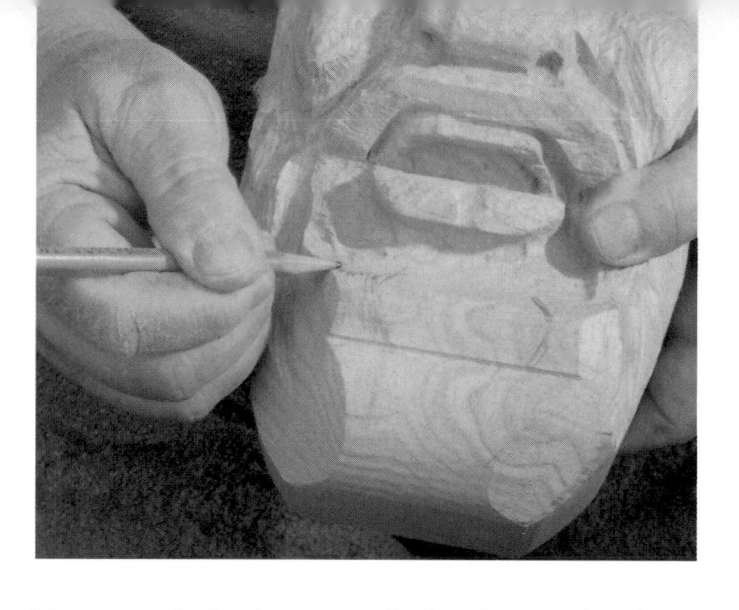

Moving on to the chin, begin to round it down, leaving it clean shaven, while the rest of the jaw line will be bearded. Mark in the location of the chin in pencil.

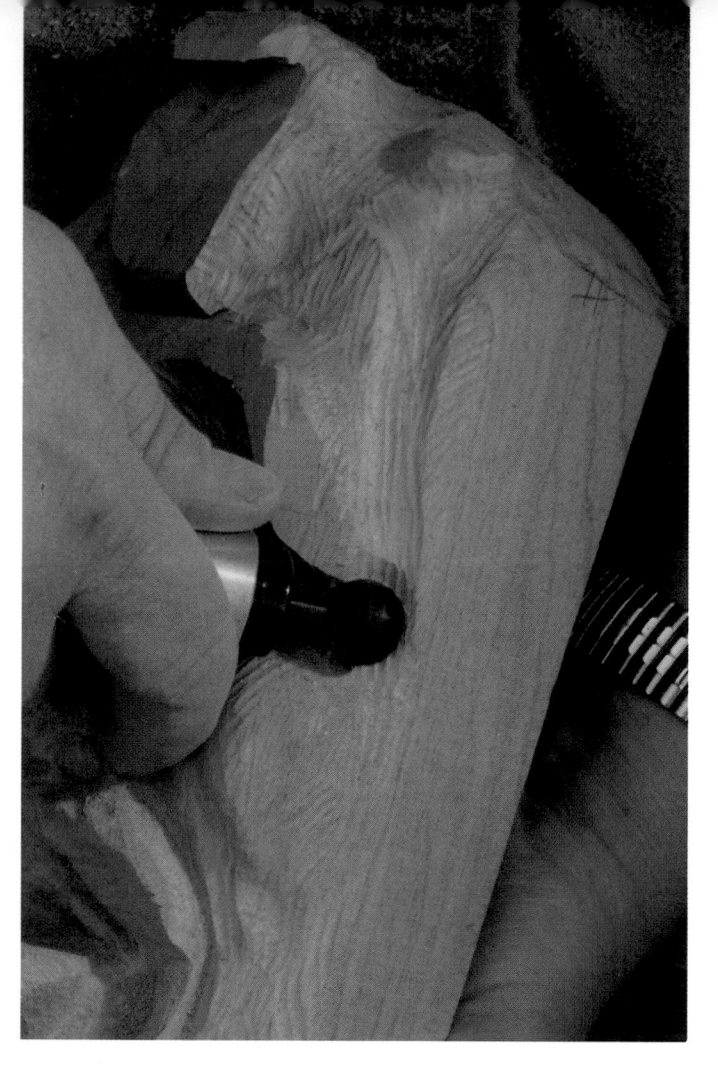

Let the hair come in around the horn and flow down into the beard. Put in a preliminary line like this first.

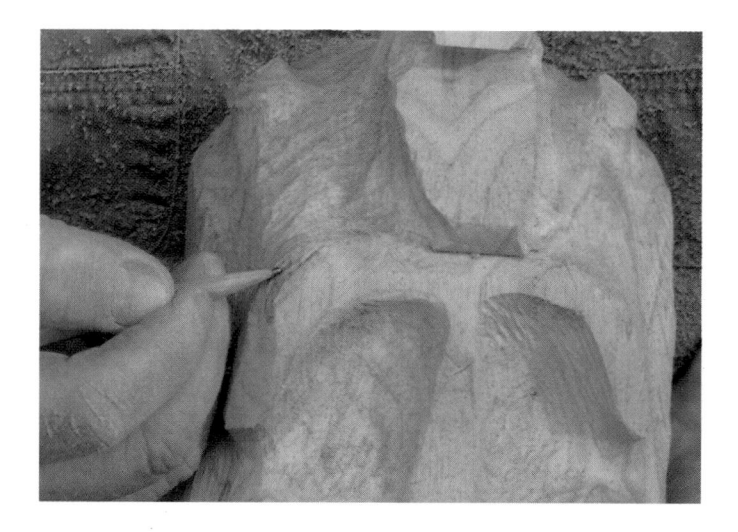

This eyebrow is too heavy. I have marked off the extra stock and will come back and remove it later.

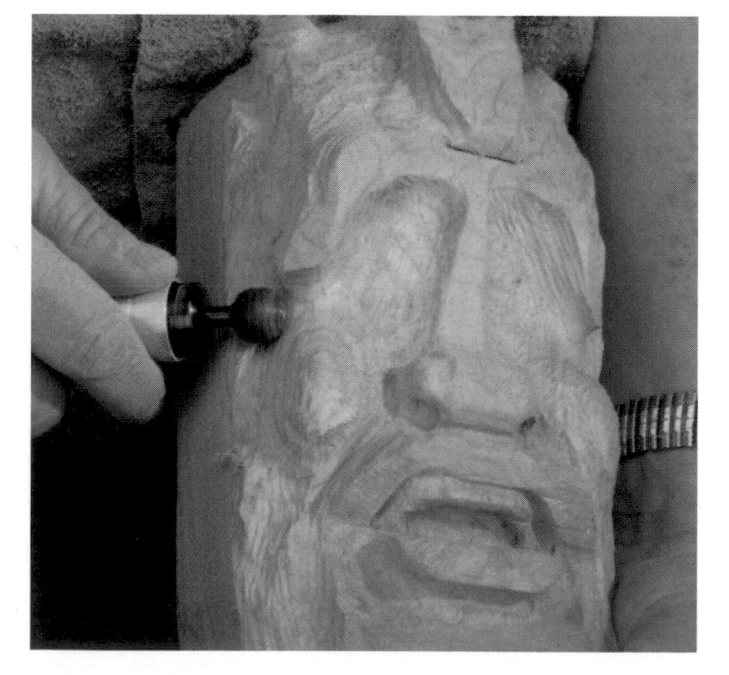

Also, while we're here, the head appears to be too wide. Deepen the lines of the temples a bit and accentuate the cheek bones to bring the shape of the head back into line.

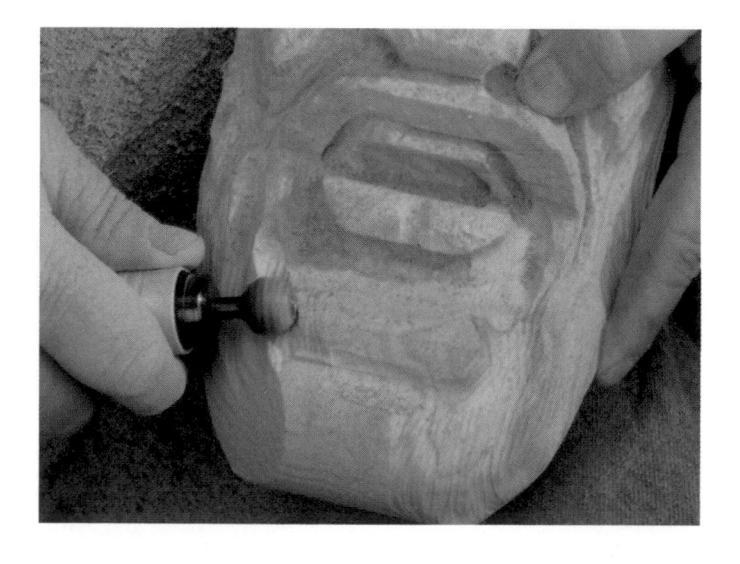

Rounding down the chin with the ball shaped Kutzall burr in the Foredom.

Progress on the chin. Note that I have added a cleft and have extended the lines of the mustache down both sides of the face to the beard beneath.

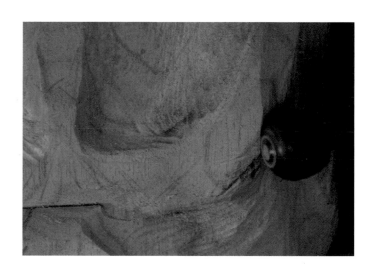

Removing the excess wood from the eyebrow.

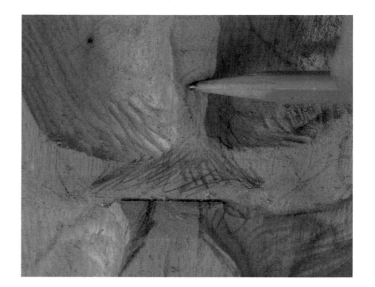

Bring the eyebrows down in the middle, where I have marked. This will give them a furrowed look.

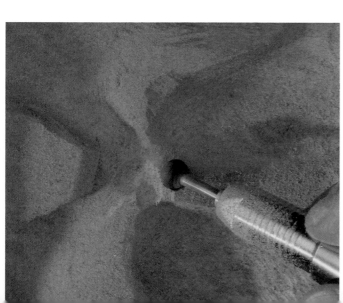

Use the small ball shaped burr in the High Tech to remove excess wood from between the eyebrows.

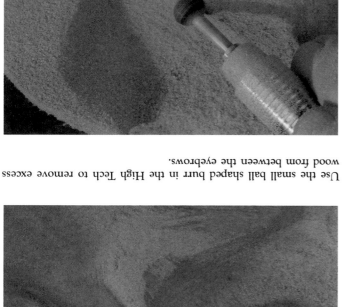

Round down the bridge of the nose some with the same burr. Once this is done, I may have to cut the eye sockets in deeper.

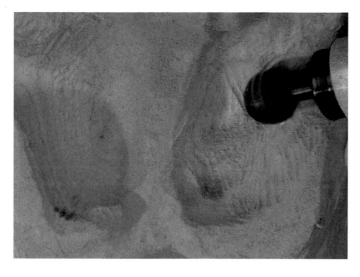

Returning to the Foredom and the large ball shaped burr, deepen the eye sockets to regain the shadows lost as we furrowed the brow and reduced the bridge of the nose.

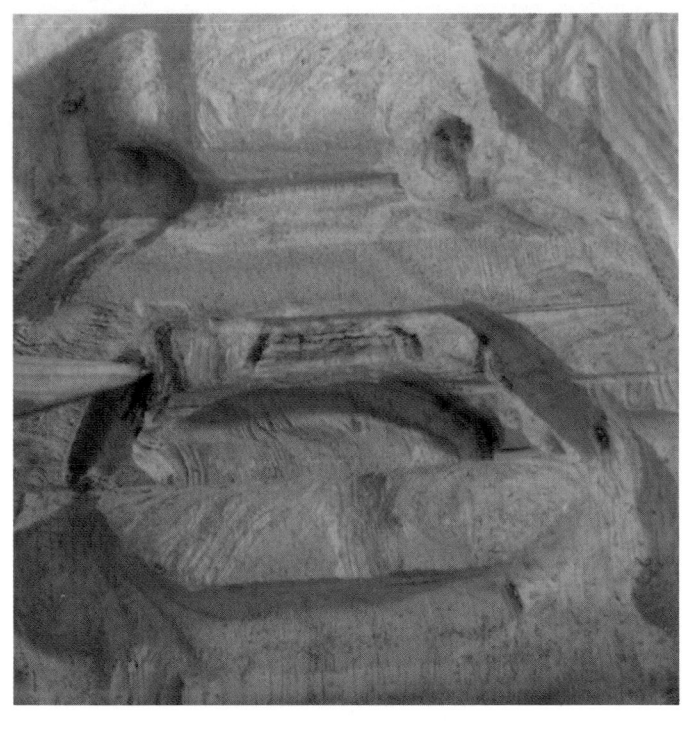

Draw in a couple of more animal looking teeth, blackening in the wood in the center to be removed.

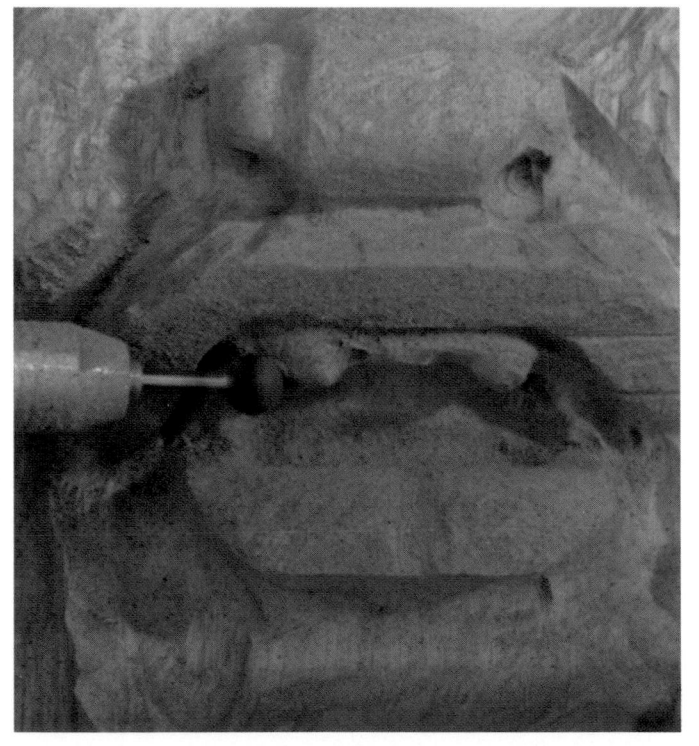

Use the small ball shaped burr in the High Tech to removed the excess wood from between and around the two canine teeth; rounding down these teeth to sharpened them.

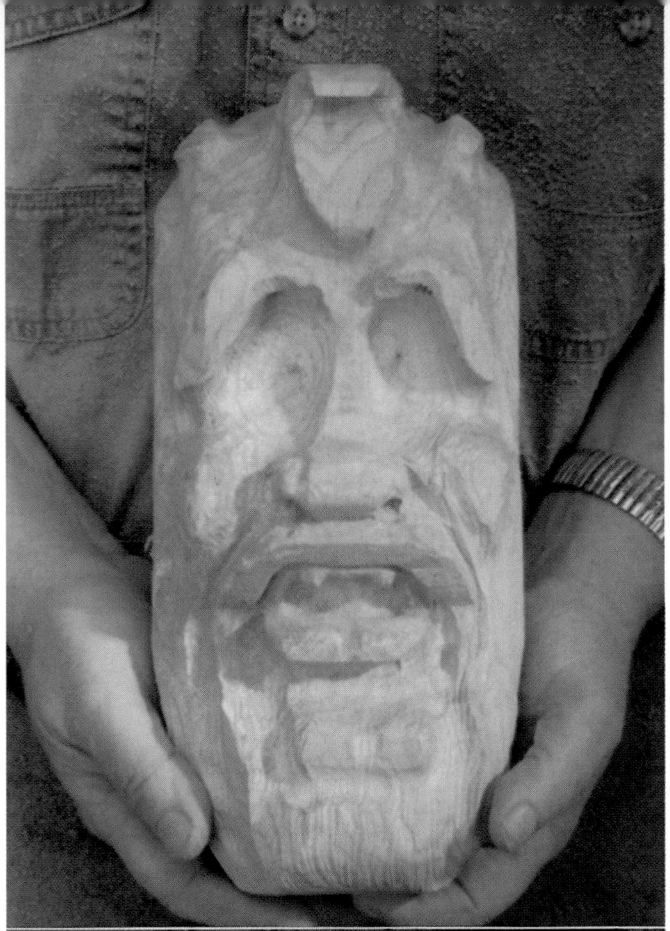

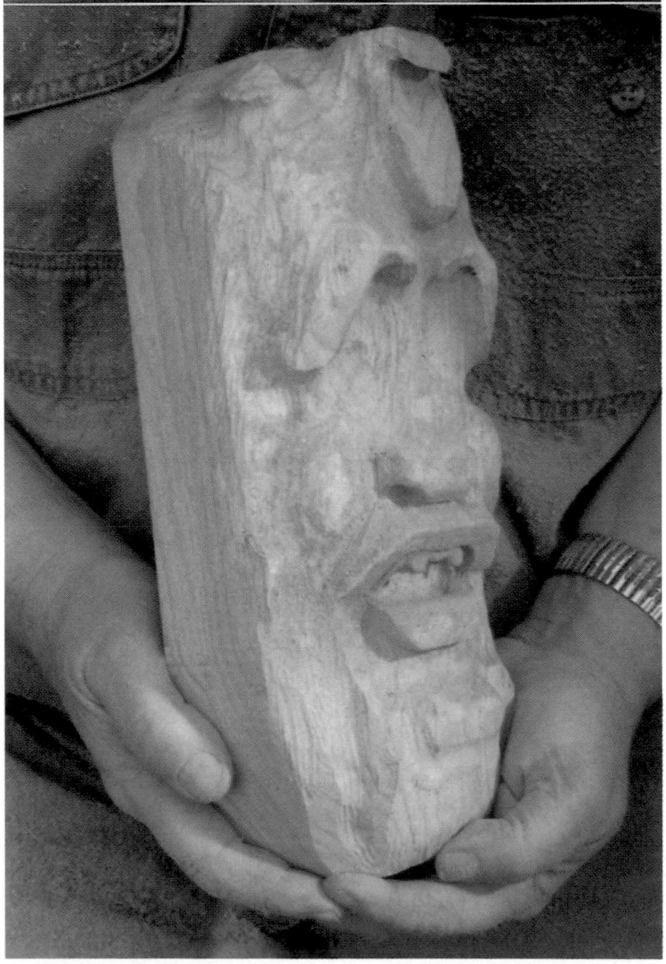

This has become a character I like more and more — a little combination of fierce and comic. I'll continue with him like this.

Moving on to a ball shaped burr to refine the detail and gain more control of the work.

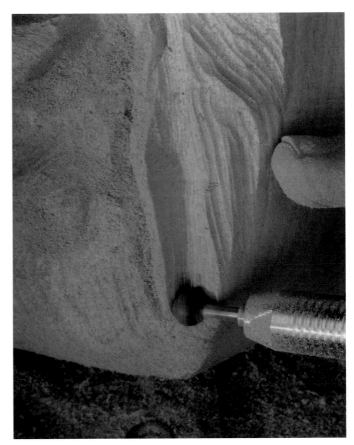

Using a more conical burr in the High Tech, I'm going to begin refining and rounding down the mustache. While doing this, I'm creating a bit of the texture of the mustache which will make it easier to finish later in the process.

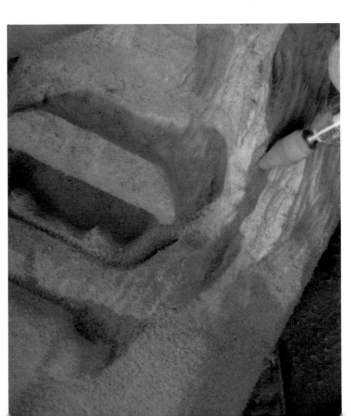

I have a problem with the chin, it is not centered under the mouth. I will round down following the pencil line to bring the chin back into line.

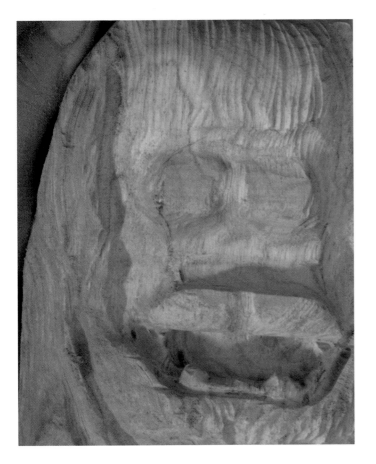

Using the small ball shaped burr I'm adding an age line extending from the corner of the eye down until it runs parallel to the line extending from the nose to the corners of the mouth and creates a fold of skin suggesting age.

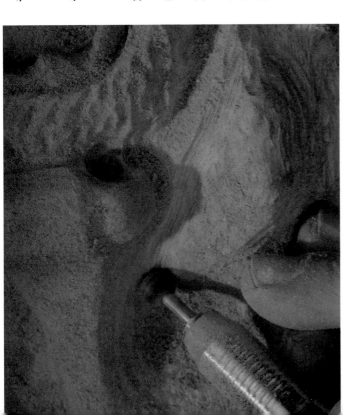

Rounding down has moved the chin over under the mouth. I also worked with the cleft until it was properly positioned as well.

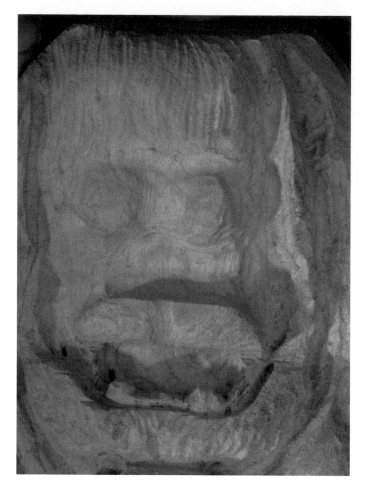

Rounding down the chin with the High Tech and the small ball shaped burr. Hopefully this will bring the chin back into line.

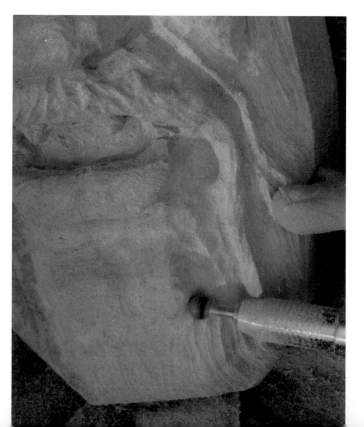

Hollowing out the top of the hairline. You can see the pencil line I am following on the other side.

I have change to a grooved cutting burr in the Foredom to see if I can get some fine stuff up here in the hair. This shape will get into some really fine curves. It is more of the cutting burr while the others I have used are grinding burrs.

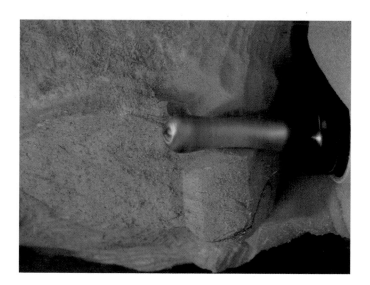

I am going to work on the hair a little bit and give it a reptilian shape that could become a serpent later. I have pencilled in the basic shape.

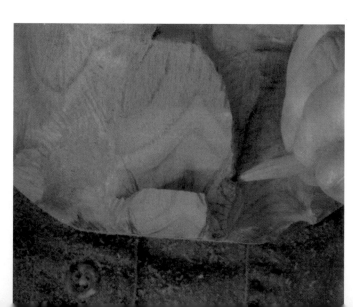

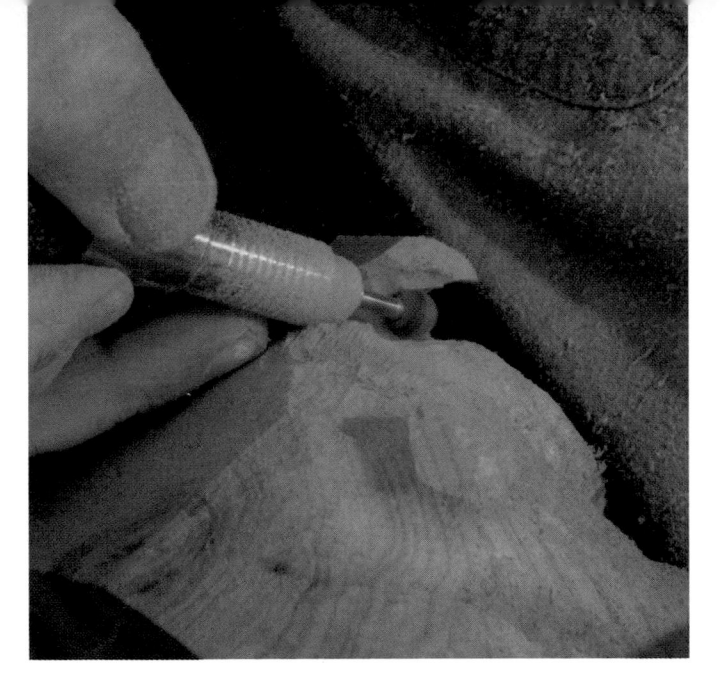

I've switched back to the High Tech with the small ball shaped burr to get some more definition into the hair.

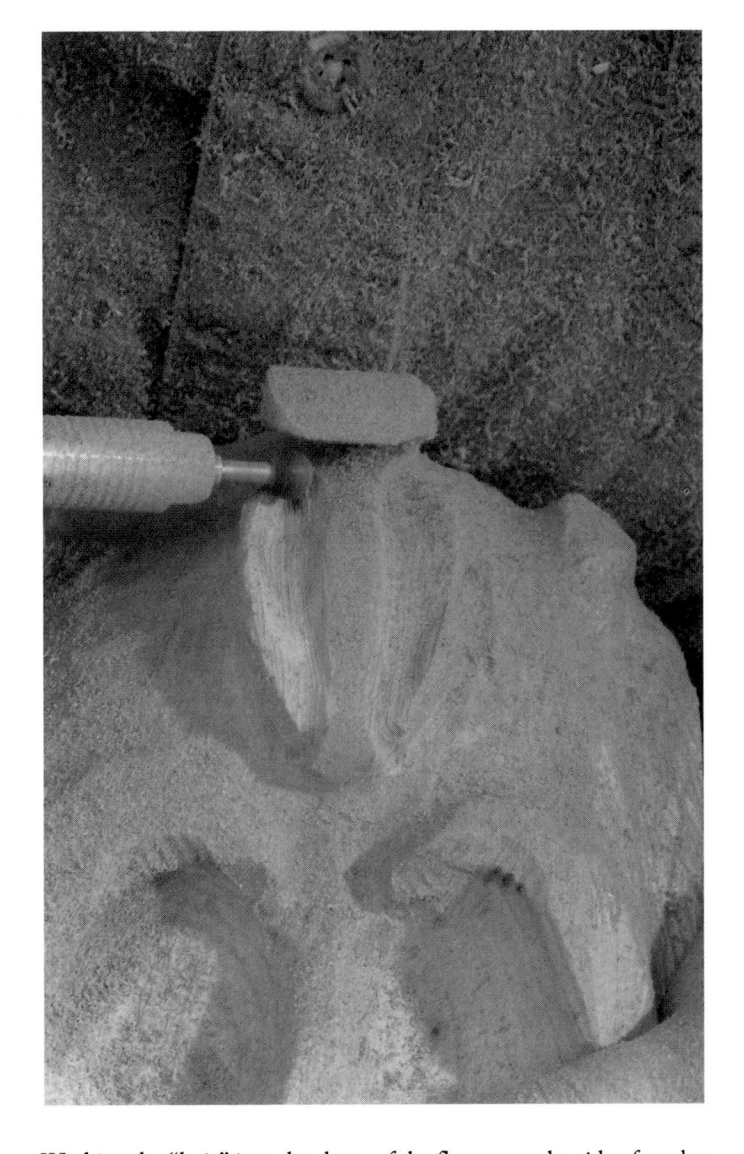

I have given the front the general heart shaped head of a cobra. Don't spend too much time trying to get this to look like a snake. This is just the general representation of a cobra ... a suggestion of the snake.

Working the "hair" into the shape of the flanges on the side of a cobra using the small ball-shaped burr. It looks good to me.

You want this to look like a button shaped horn coming out of a swelled up place in the skin. Like this.

Go around the button with the small ball shaped burr in the High Tech and then again higher on the button itself.

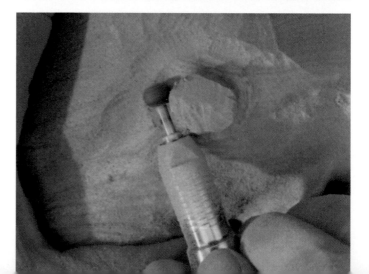

This burr is also good for increasing the depth of the hair lines themselves. This is where we take advantage of the line that were already there, the ones we made earlier.

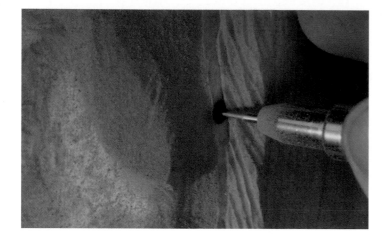

Switching back to the first head on the High Tech and using an even smaller burr, a disk shaped cutting burr, smooth down the surfaces, and create the fine separations between the skin and the hair. Use as light a touch as possible with this burr. You don't want burn marks.

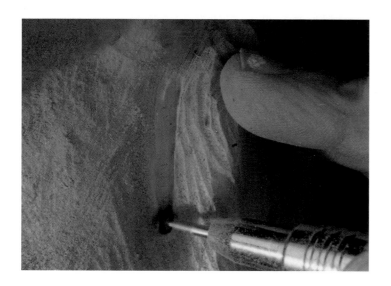

Using a finer cone shaped cutting burr on the Foredom, undercut the edges of the snake shaped hair to provide greater definition.

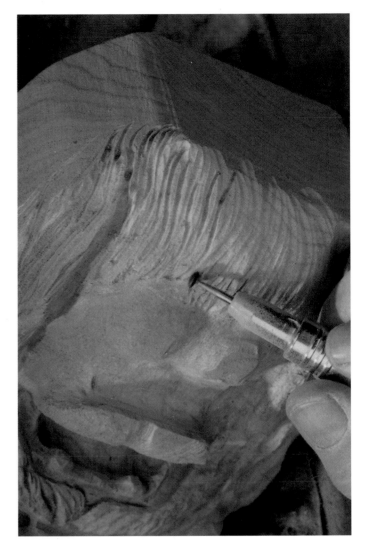

Refining the hair in the beard as well.

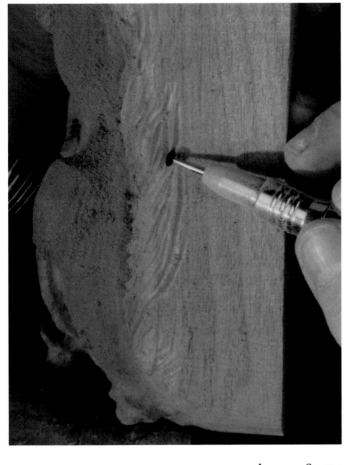

Bring the hair down around the side so that the head will appear finished right down to where it meets the side panels.

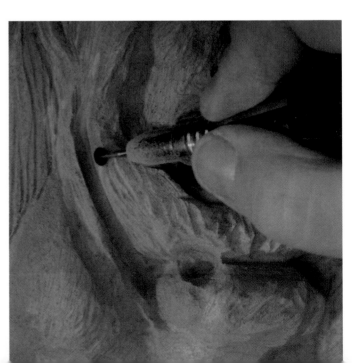

Refining the lines of the face and the mustache. I'm taking advantage of the lines that are already there everywhere I can.

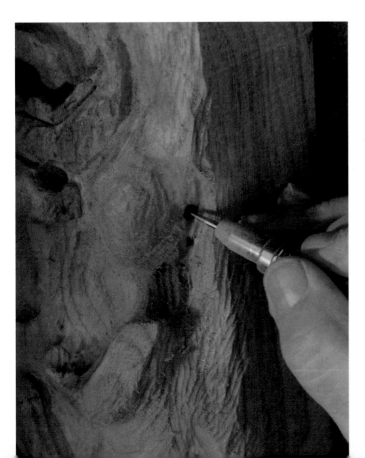

Cutting in the separation between the cheek and the beard.

Extending and refining the hair on the side of the head. Note the clear separation between hair and skin.

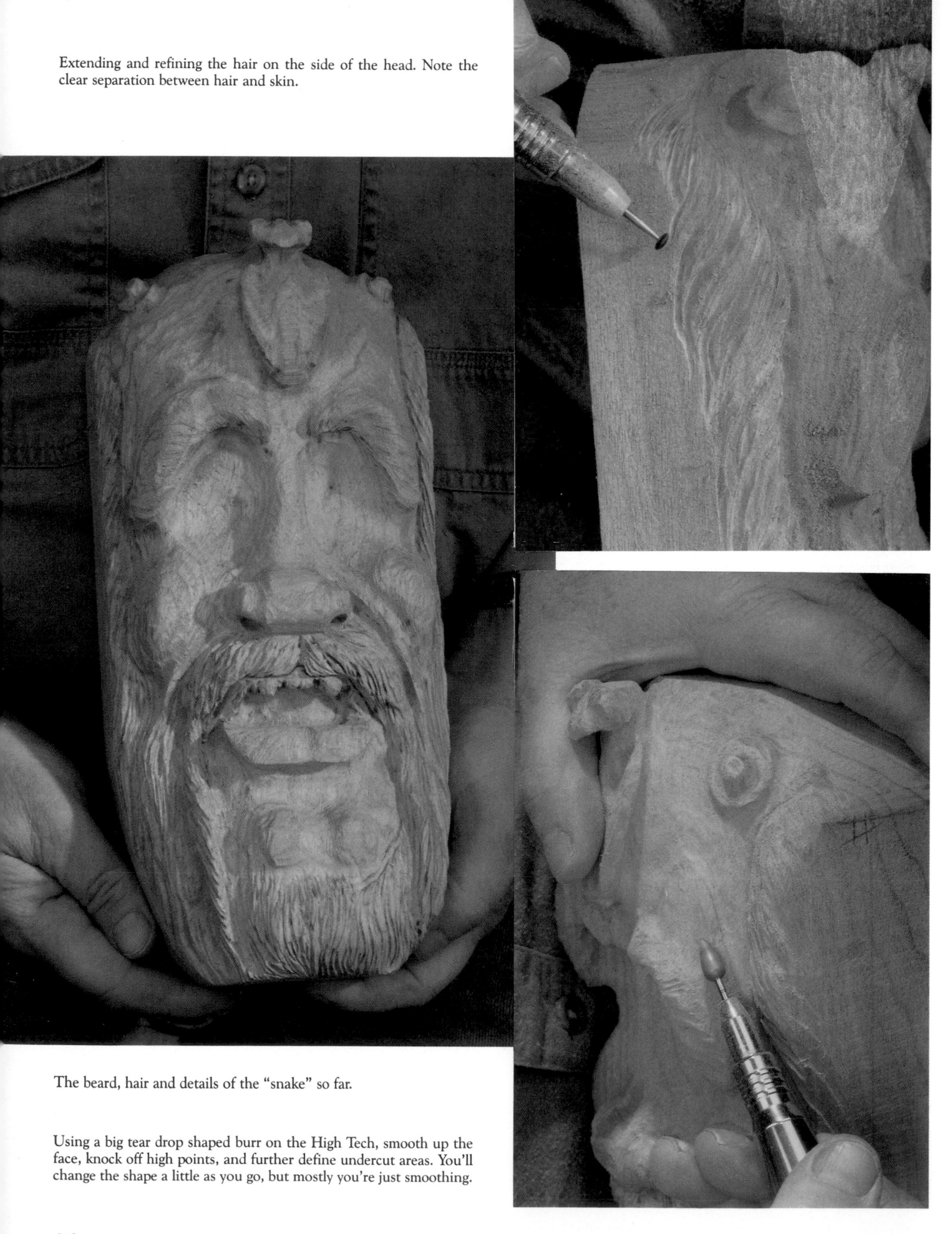

The beard, hair and details of the "snake" so far.

Using a big tear drop shaped burr on the High Tech, smooth up the face, knock off high points, and further define undercut areas. You'll change the shape a little as you go, but mostly you're just smoothing.

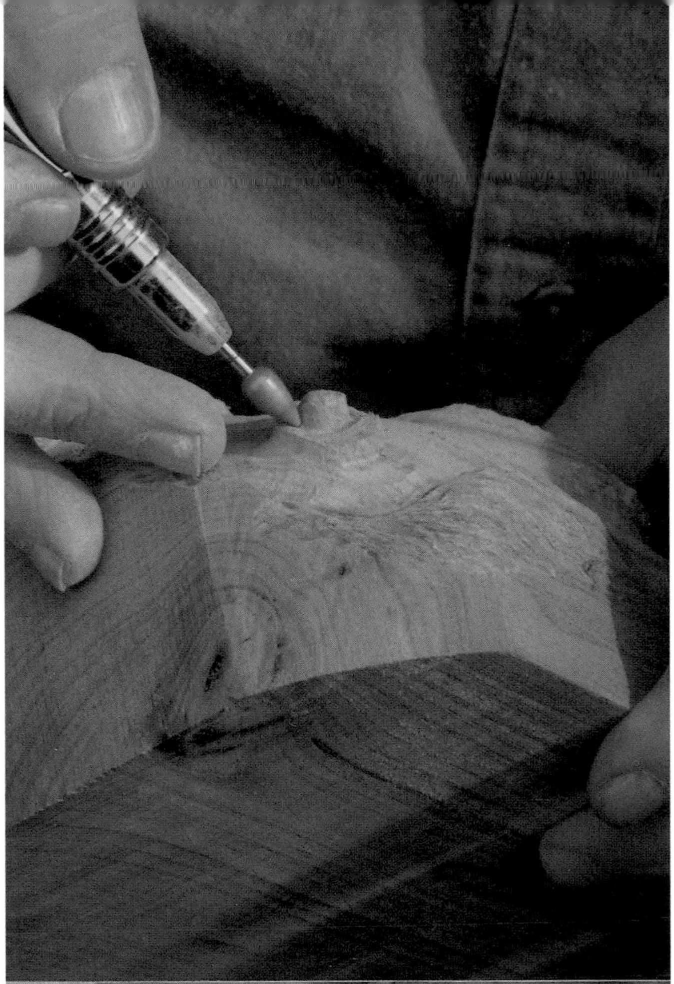

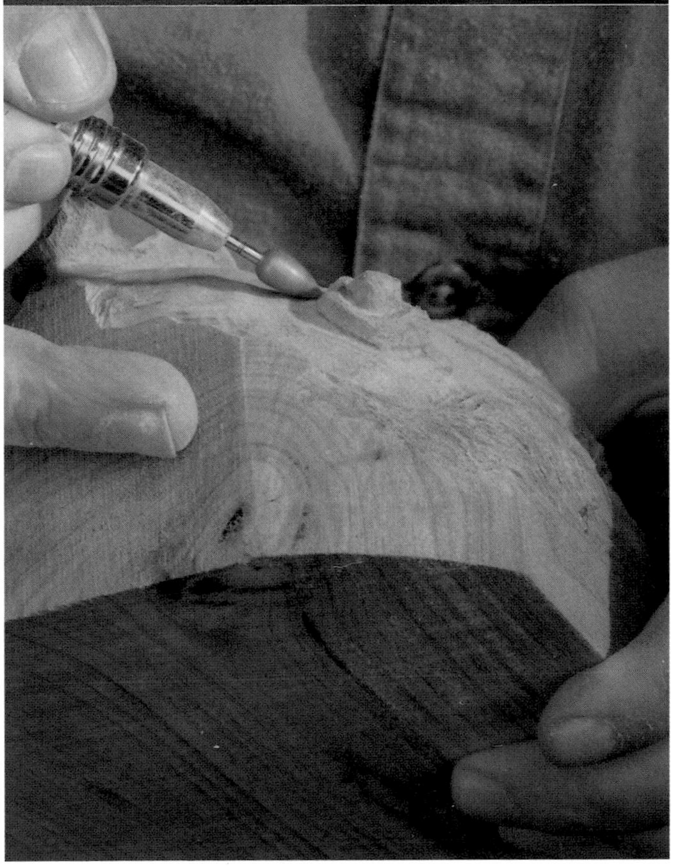

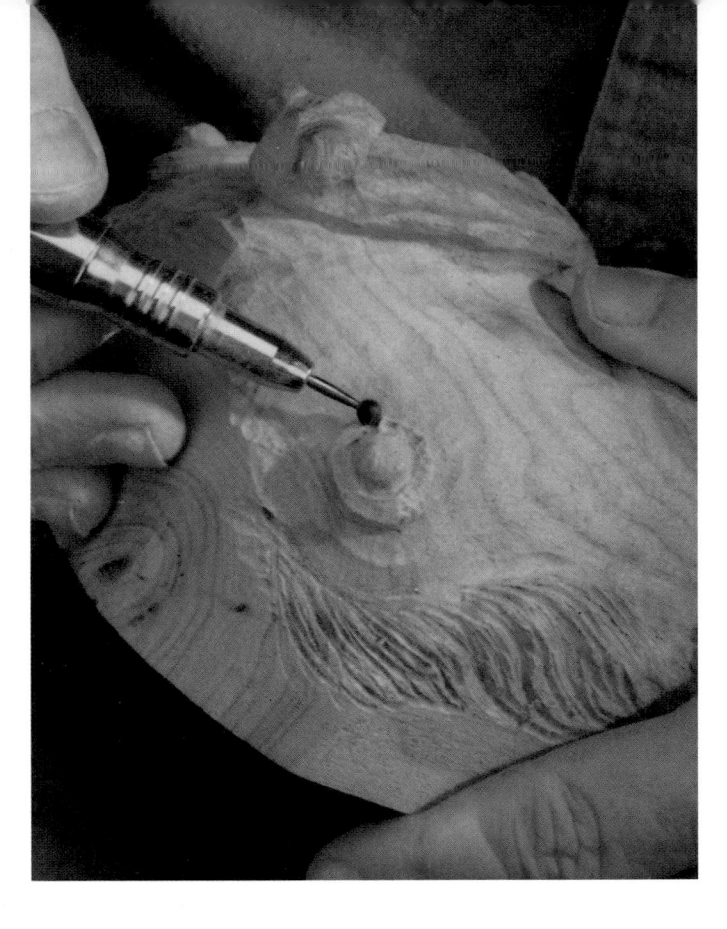

Change to a smaller round ruby bit to finish around the horns. Use this bit to pucker the skin in a series of vertical cuts. The horns will appear to have burst up through the skin here.

This is a ruby point. It's good for sanding and refining the shapes. The ruby will actually cut more than the diamond will. This ruby cone shaped burr is being used to refine the details around the horns.

The finished horn.

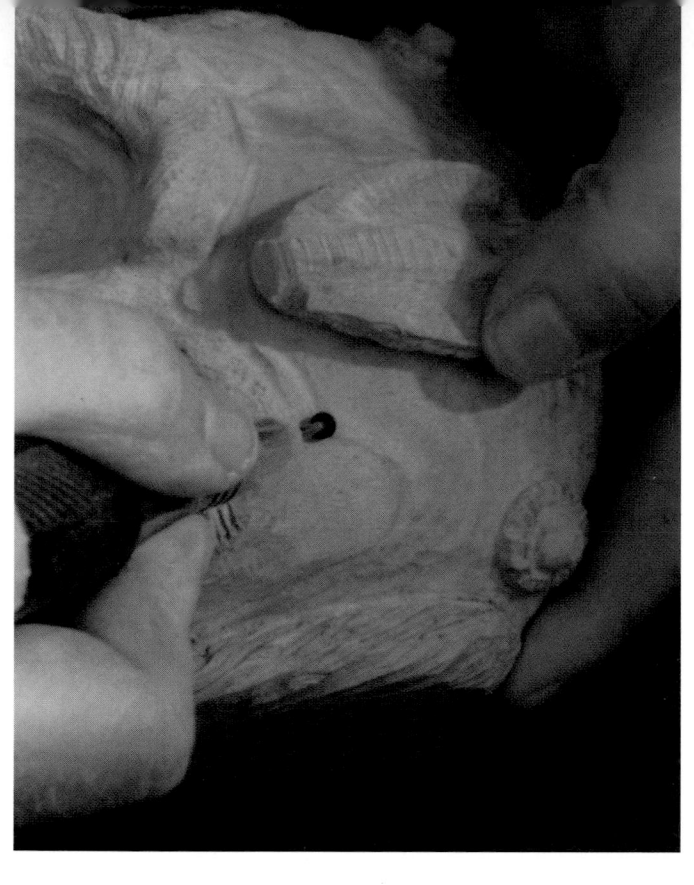

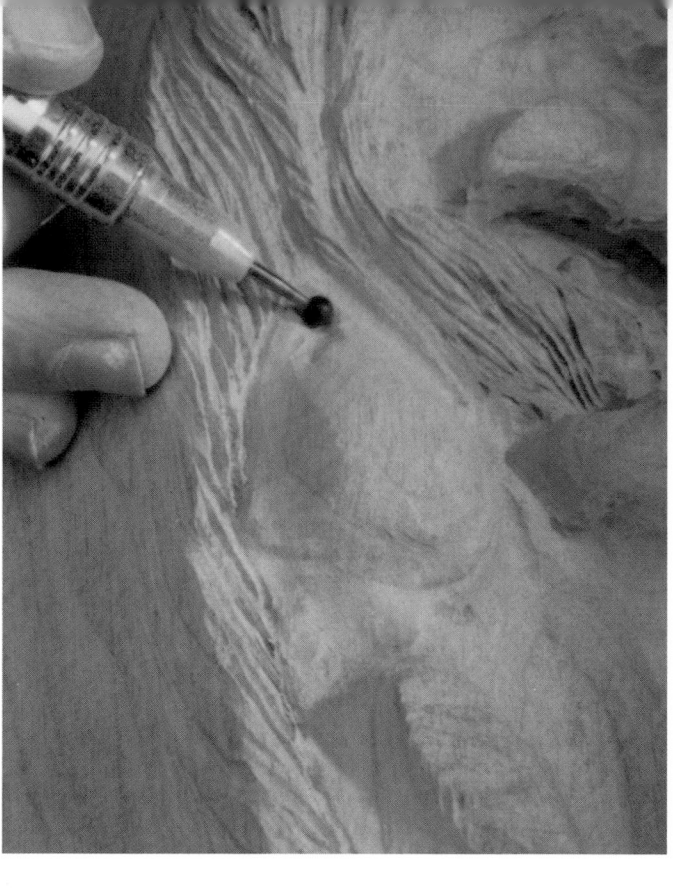

Use the small ball shaped burr in the High Tech to add expression lines to the forehead and odd bumps and wrinkles. This begins to transform him from something human into something more animalistic.

Add some depth to the base of the cheeks for expression. These are the details that change a good carving into a great one. Also, think about gargoyles when making these house spirits. Give them those odd animalistic features, adding interest to your work.

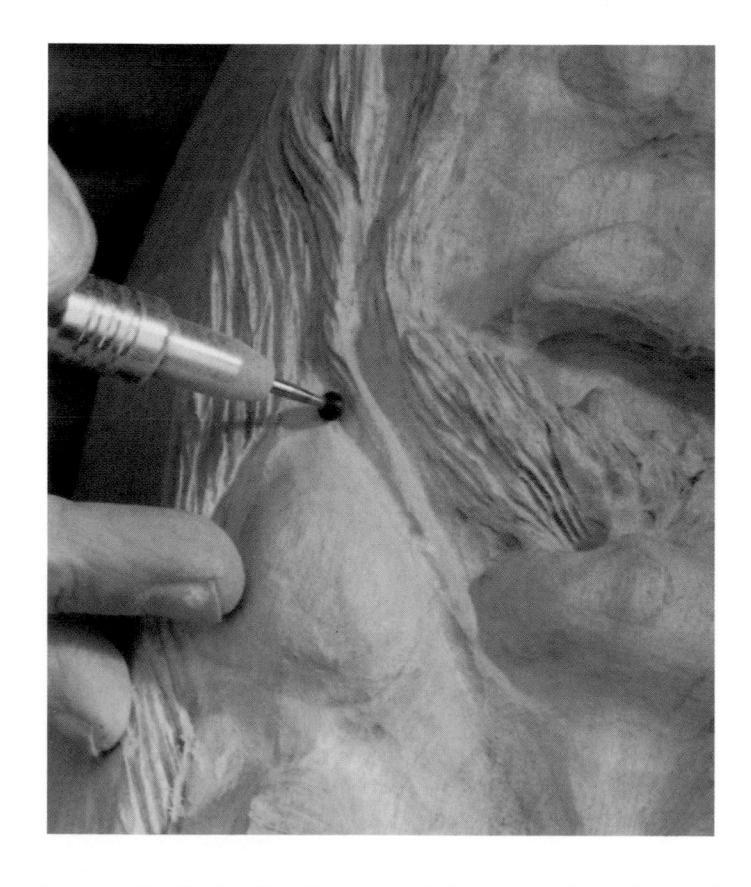

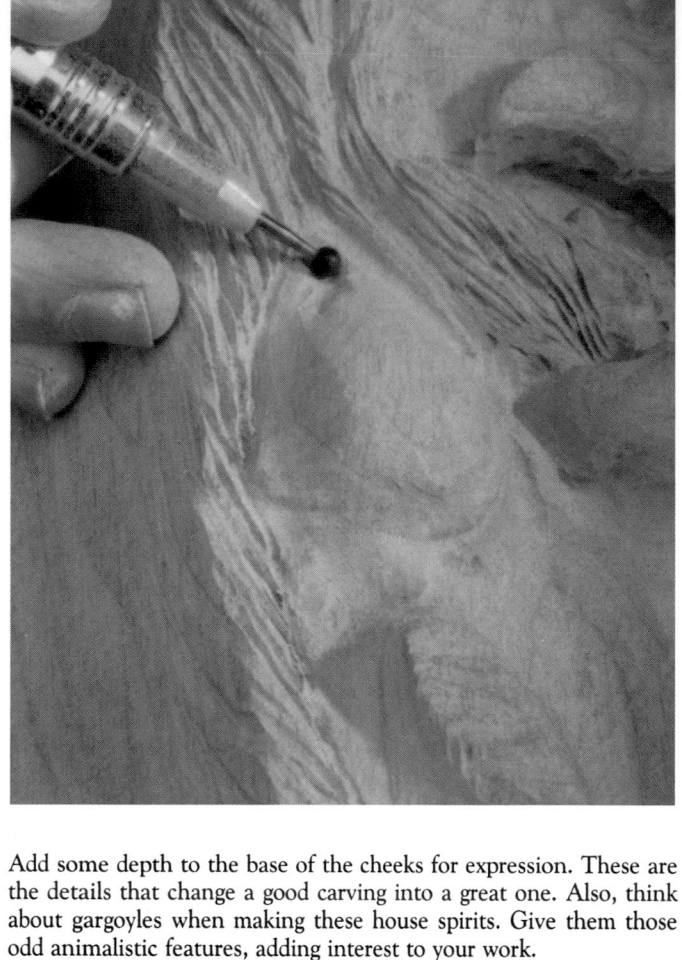

Increase the depth of the lines around the nose and mouth to add more character. The more detail you can add from here on out, the better your carving will be.

Add these little louvers to the snake-like feature to give it more character.

I am using a ball shaped diamond burr in the High Tech to take down the extra wood around the inside edge of this eye. A ruby burr would have been better but this was what I had with me. Be careful, the diamond burr tends to burn a little, but small strokes will remove the burn.

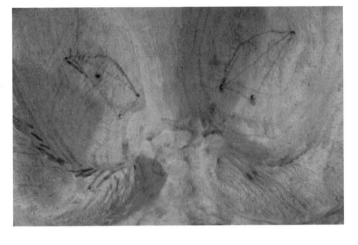

These are the cutting lines around the eyes. The heavy dots of the measuring points will also give you a key as to where to begin your knife strokes.

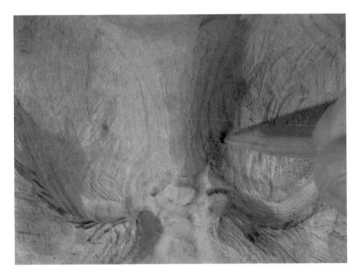

You need both eye sockets to be as close to symmetrical as you can make them. This marked in area needs to come down more.

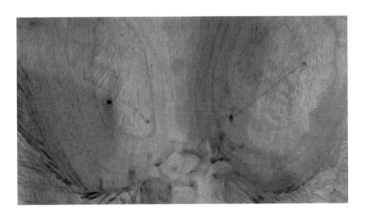

These are only measuring lines. They give you the angle of the eyes and the size. Don't think of these as anything as you would cut on.

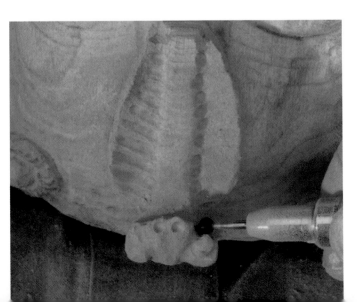

Adding nostrils and eyeballs to this beastie on the house spirit's forehead. Whatever it is, it shouldn't be viewed after dark.

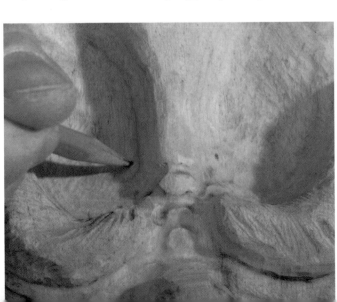

This is the inside tear duct. That location, in a way, tells you about the size of the eye. You should have five eye spaces across the head (a rule of thumb for a believable character). The distance between the inside corners should give you the distance of the eyeballs themselves. This is not written in blood but you do want your figure to look realistic.

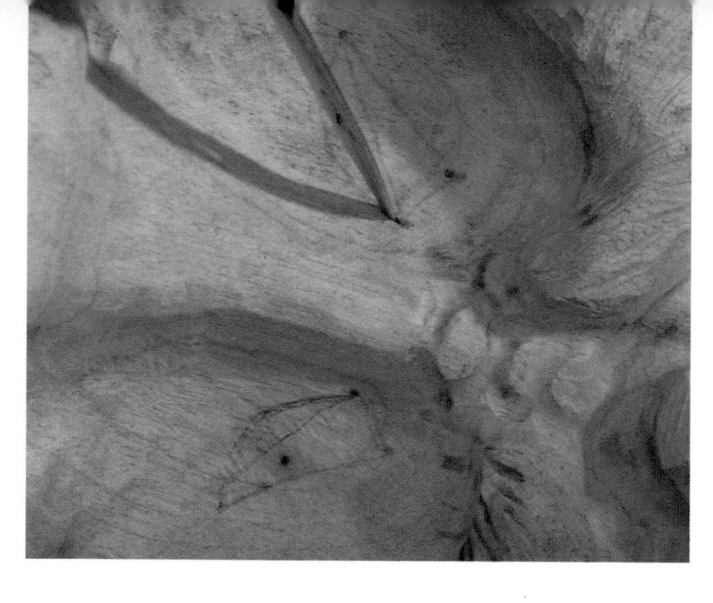

The eyes can be done with either a rotary tool or a pocket knife. We'll do one with each. This is a Case pocket knife. I have altered the blades to suit myself. Make the first cut along one side of the inside measuring point, following the shape of the lower eyelid.

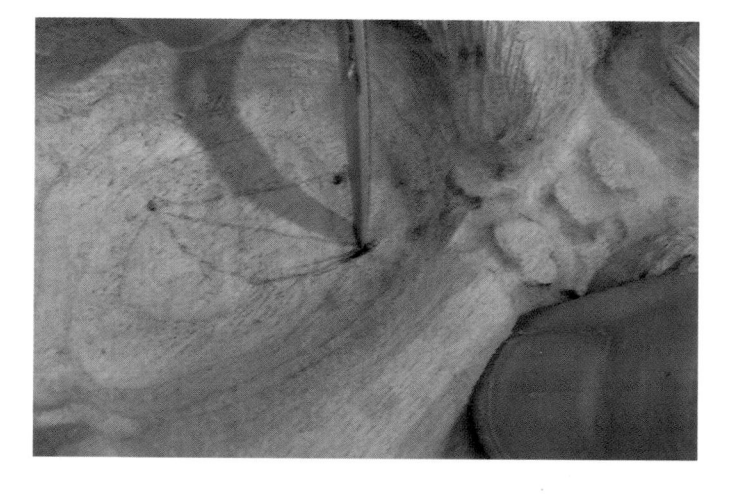

Make another cut, straight in as before along the upper eyelid in this corner.

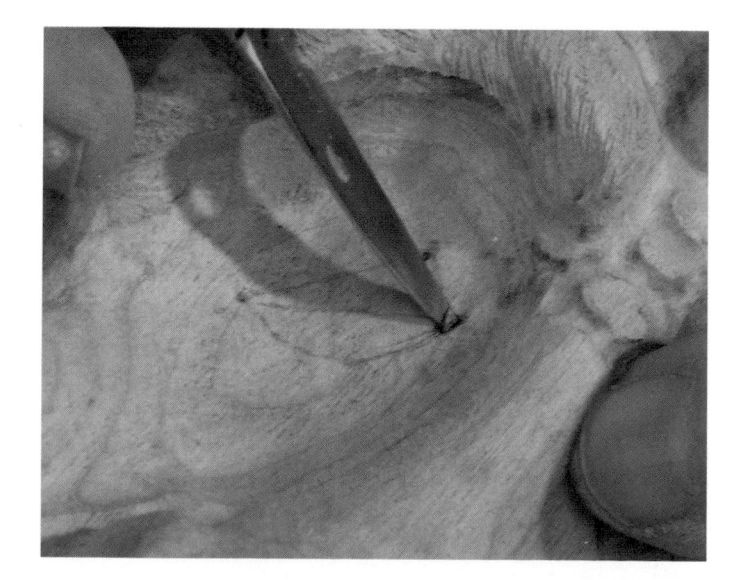

Cut out the corner where they meet, creating a shallow depression along the inside edge of the eye.

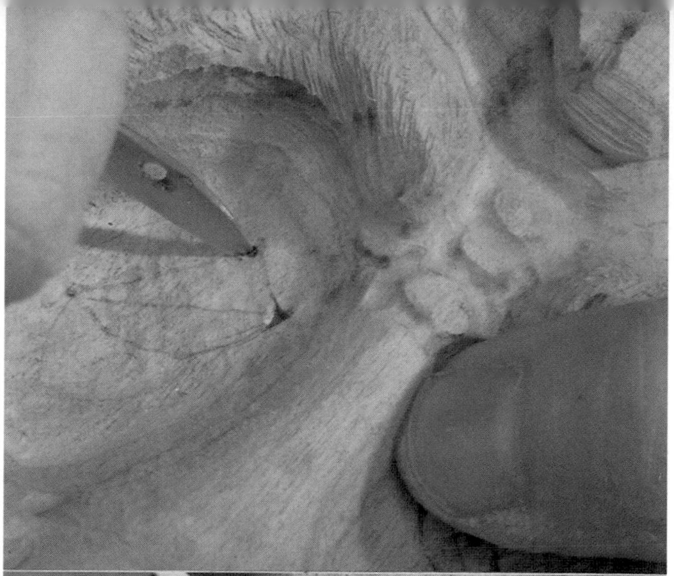

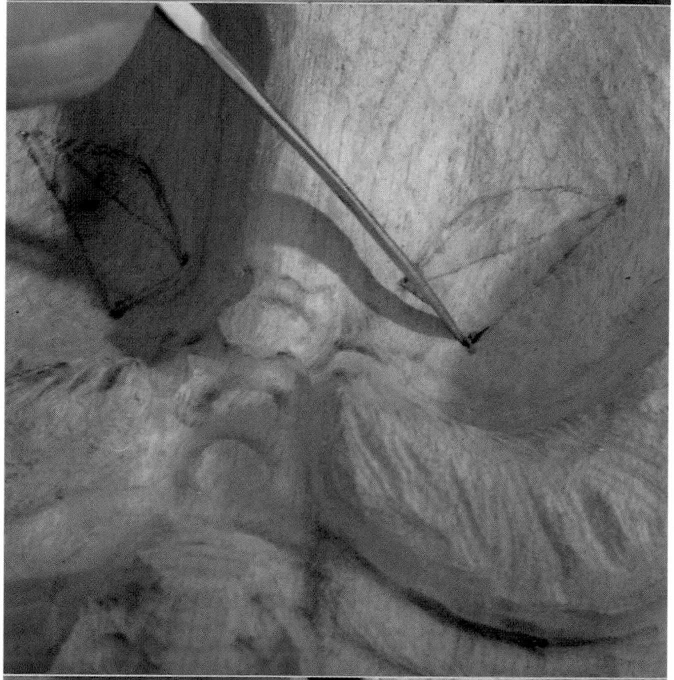

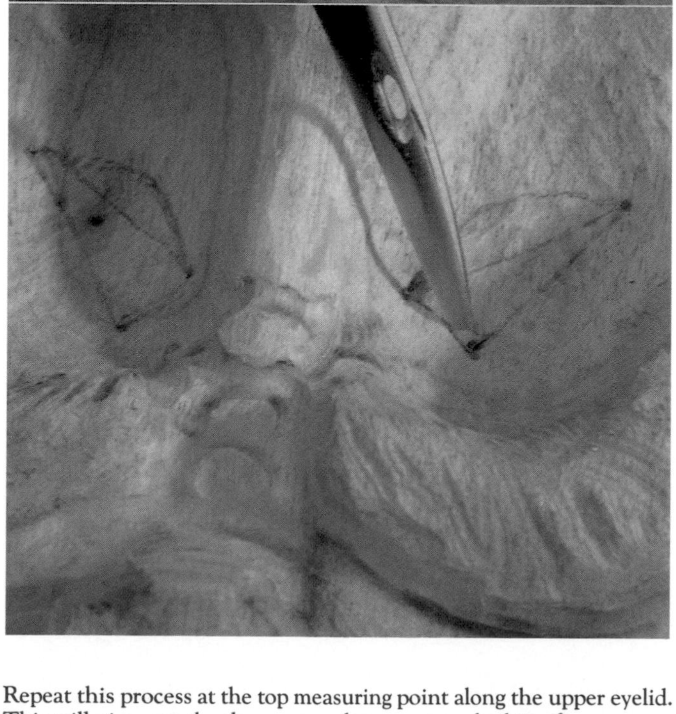

Repeat this process at the top measuring point along the upper eyelid. This will give you the droopy eye shape you are looking for.

Make shallow stop cuts straight in along the lines of the eyes.

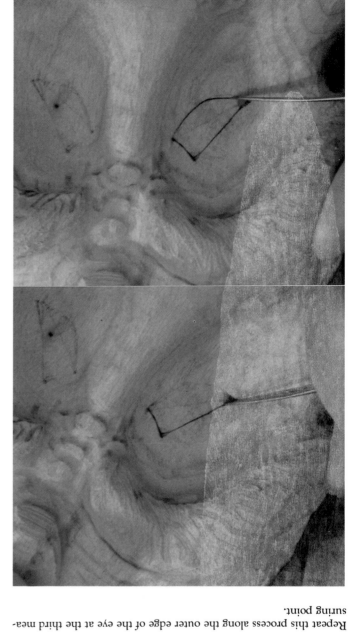

Repeat this process along the outer edge of the eye at the third measuring point.

The rounded eye.

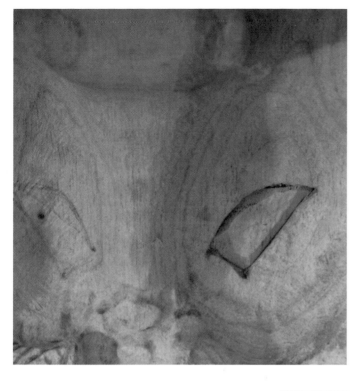

Now cut back in at an angle to the stop cut lines to give the eyeball a rounded look.

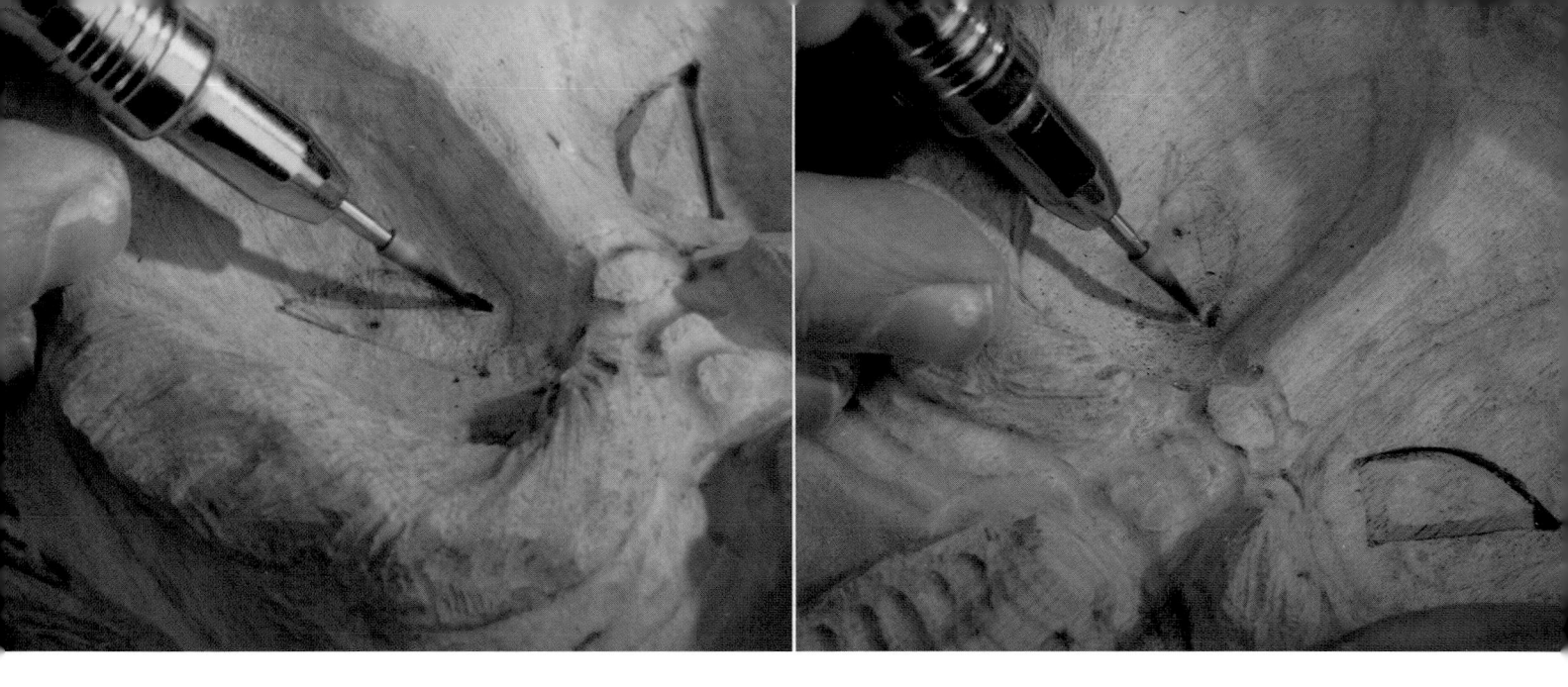

Moving on to the other eye, carving it out with the High Tech rotary power tool. Using a long, small pinpoint diamond burr, repeat the cuts you made in the measuring points of the other eye. The technique is just about the same.

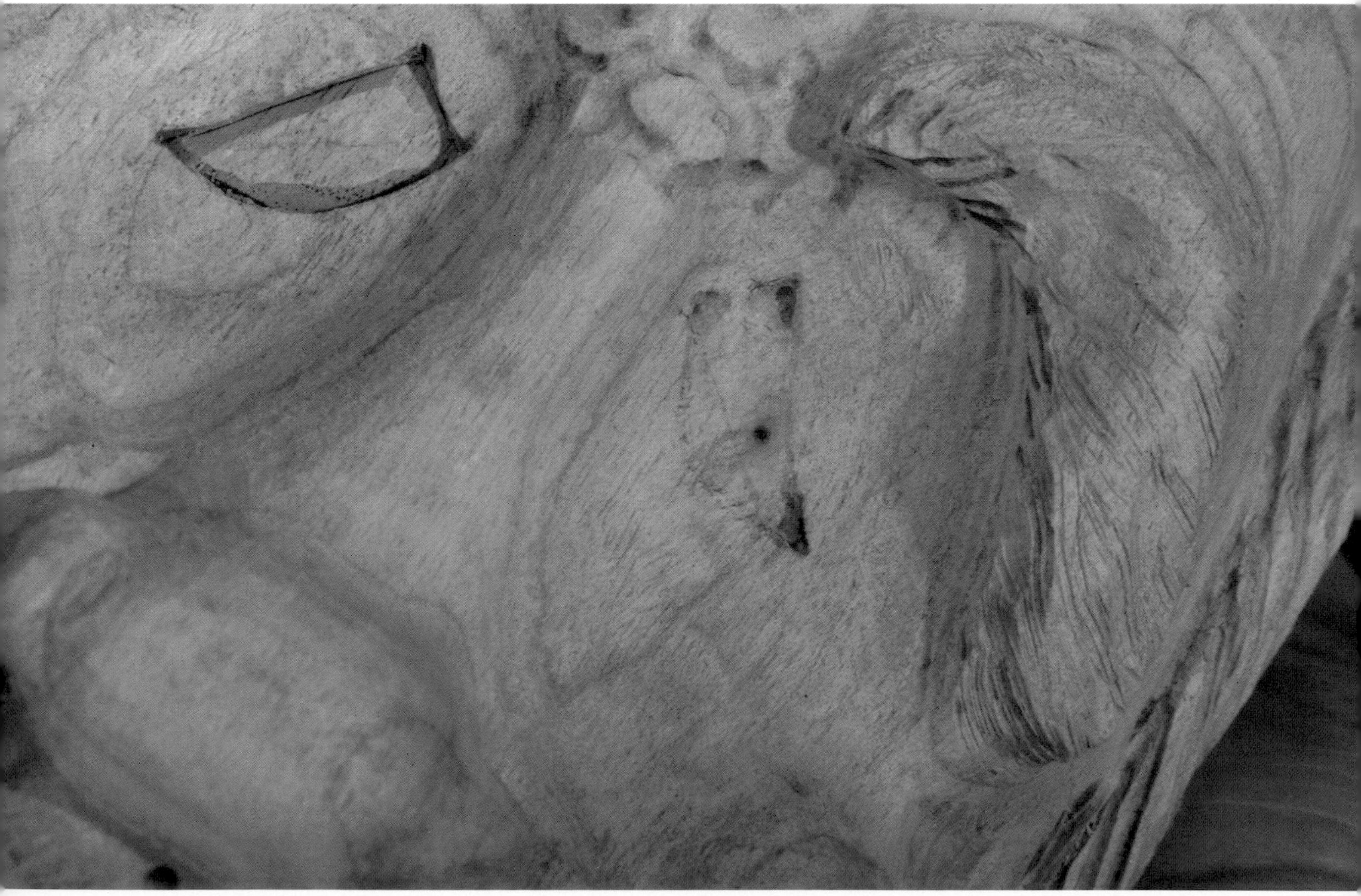

Repeat the process at all three measuring points as before.

Follow along the edges of the eye as before. As you can see, the hand carved eye is a little neater at this point. It is also a little larger.

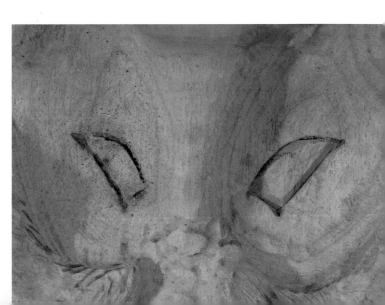

I will enlarge the rotary carved eye with my knife and clean up the work a bit as well.

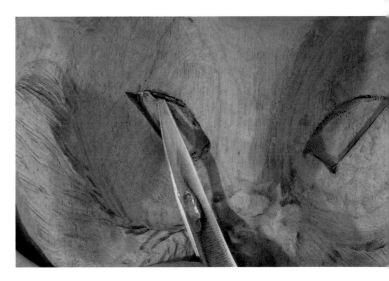

Use a small disk in the High Tech to dress up the eyeball. This refines the shape of the eyeball. It also undercuts the eyeball a bit and makes it more realistic.

Using a little, round burr I am going to carve in the eyelids. First sketch the lines in with a pencil. Begin with the lines of the drooping upper eyelid.

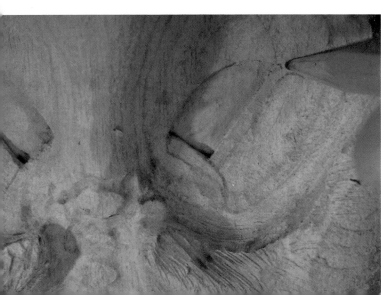

Sketch in the lower lid as well. Keep the lines in close enough to the eyes to keep the lower lid from looking like a bag. Also leave the outer edges of the lids open in the shape of crows feet.

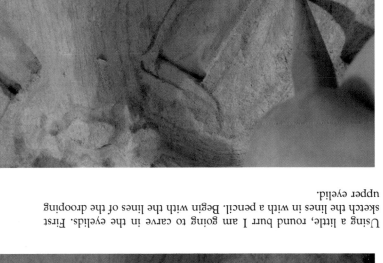

Use the High Tech with the small round burr to cut out carefully along the lines of the eyelids. Be careful not to break the lid.

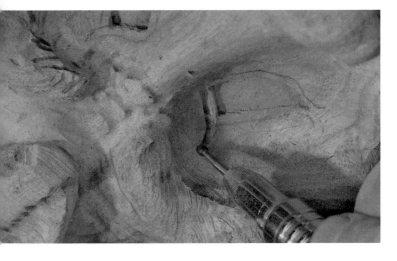

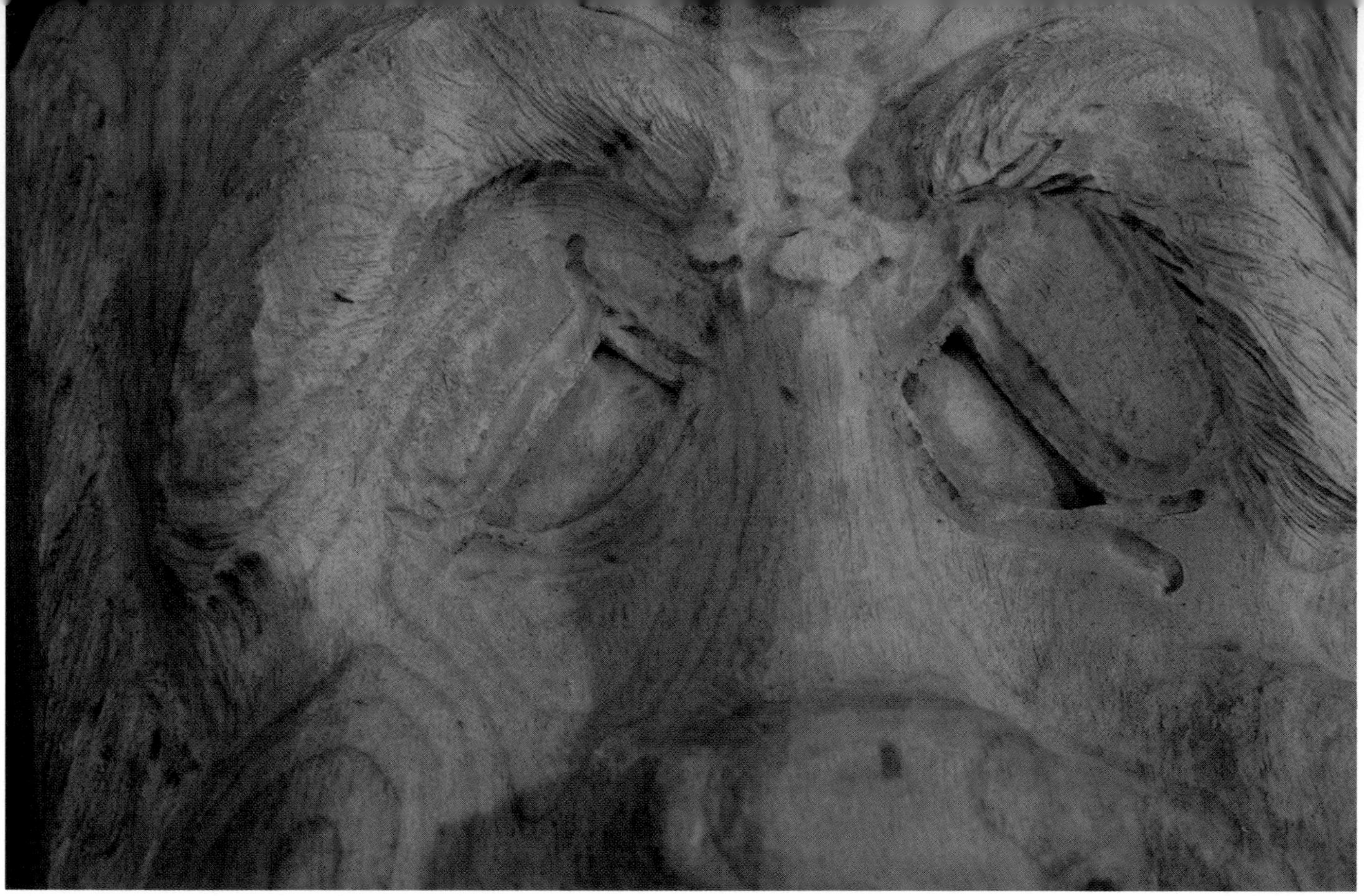

The eyelid lines.

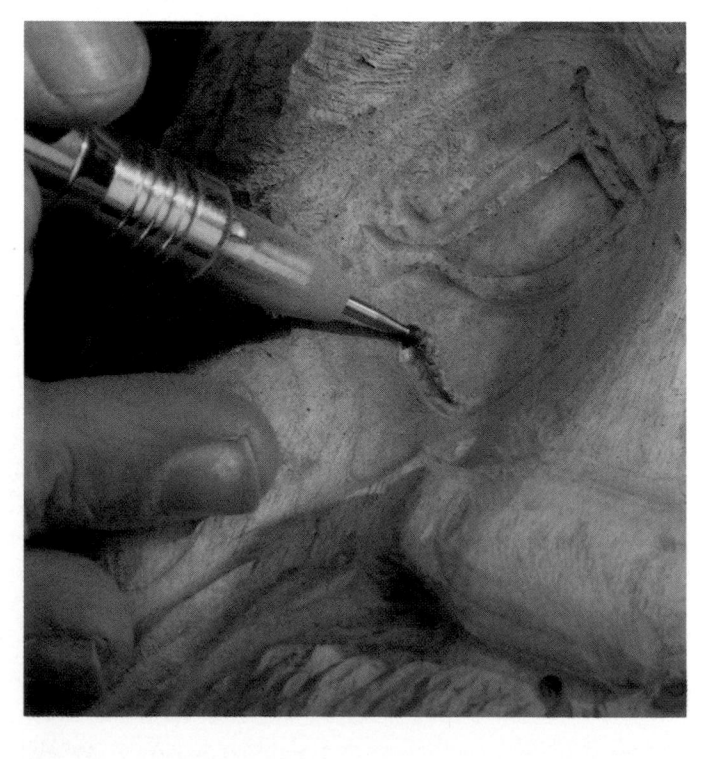

Using the same burr, place a bag under each eye. Outline the bags under the eyes first.

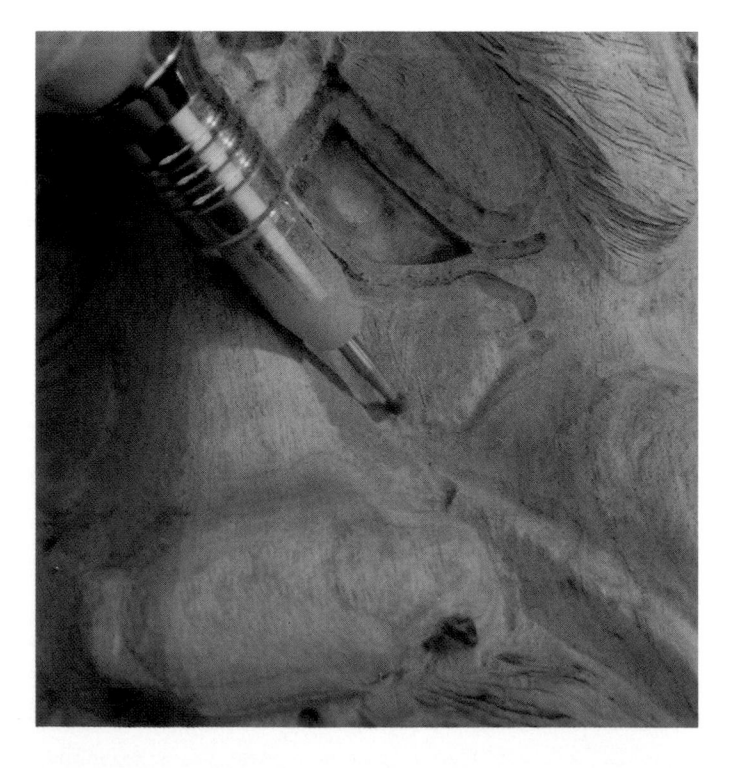

Round down the surface of the bag above and below the outline, eliminating the sharp outline edges.

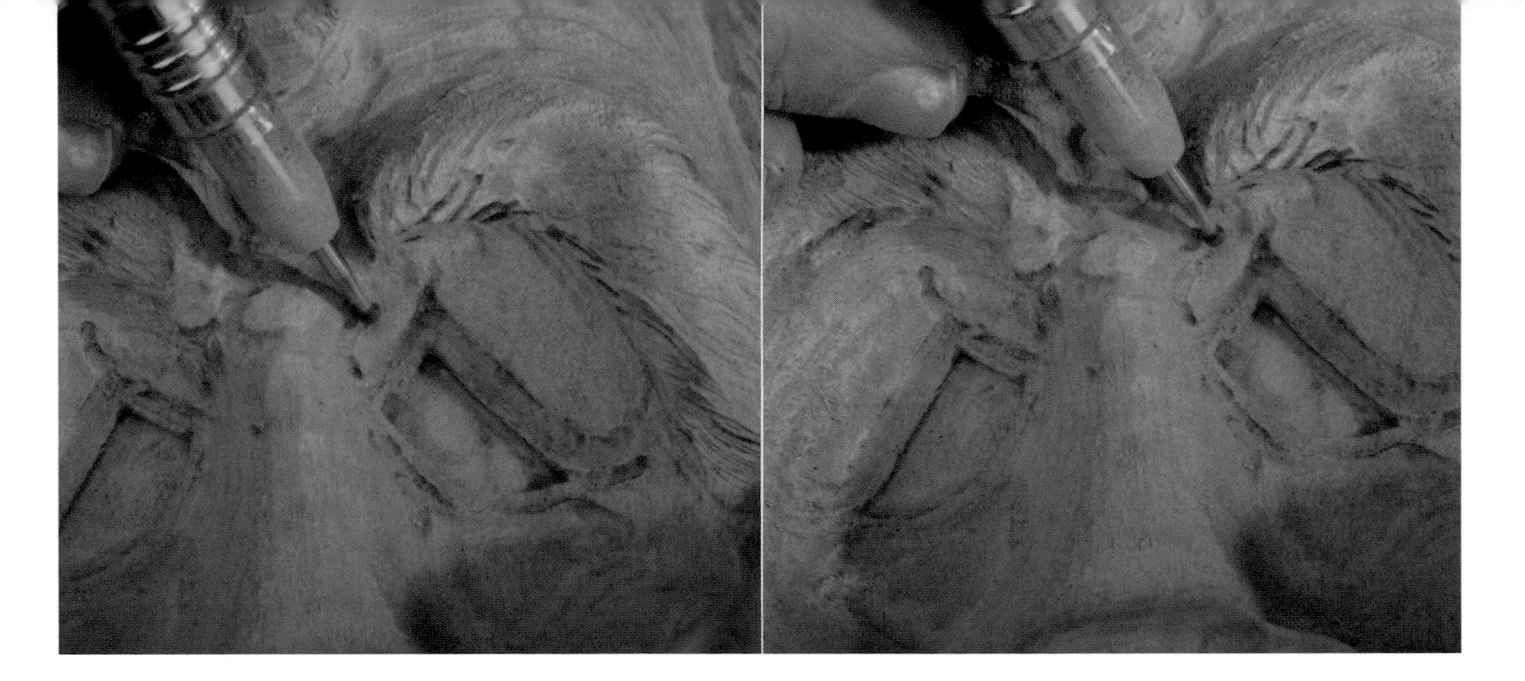

Put in some knots and gnarls around the eyes to show age and take away some of the human appearance, giving the house spirit a more gargoyle-ish look.

Here is an early idea of what the piece will look like all together.

The cheeks do not match up right. I have marked in the area that needs to be removed. I will use the round Kutzall burr to reduce this marked cheek to try to match it to the other cheek.

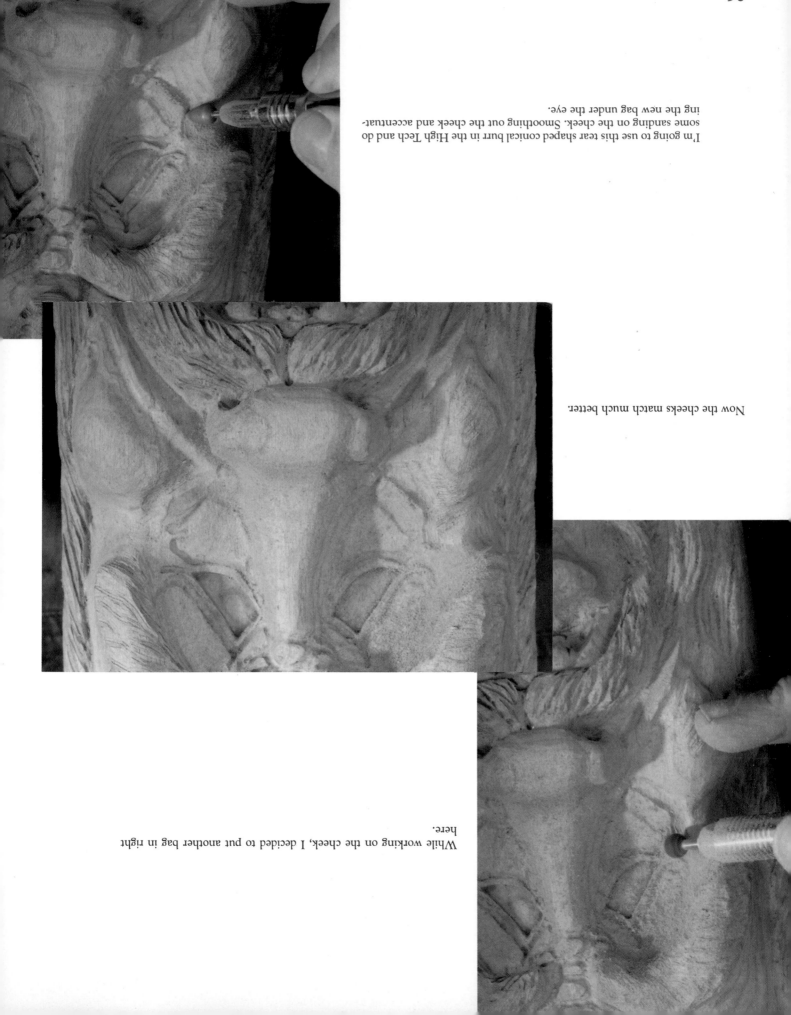

I'm going to use this tear shaped conical burr in the High Tech and do some sanding on the cheek. Smoothing out the cheek and accentuating the new bag under the eye.

Now the cheeks match much better.

While working on the cheek, I decided to put another bag in right here.

WE HOPE THAT YOU ENJOY THIS BOOK . . . and that it will occupy a proud place in your library. We would like to keep you informed about other publications from Schiffer Publishing Ltd.

TITLE OF BOOK: _____

☐ hardcover
☐ paperback

☐ Bought at: _____
☐ Received as gift

COMMENTS: _____

_____

_____

Name *(please print clearly)* _____

Address _____

City _____ State _____ Zip _____

☐ *Please send me a free Schiffer Arts, Antiques & Collectibles catalog.*
☐ *Please send me a free Schiffer Woodcarving, Woodworking & Crafts catalog*
☐ *Please send me a free Schiffer Military/Aviation History catalog*
☐ *Please send me a free Whitford Press Mind, Body & Spirit and Donning Pictorials &*
   *Cookbooks catalog.*

SCHIFFER BOOKS ARE CURRENTLY AVAILABLE FROM YOUR BOOKSELLER

SCHIFFER PUBLISHING LTD
77 LOWER VALLEY RD
ATGLEN PA 19310-9717

PLACE
STAMP
HERE

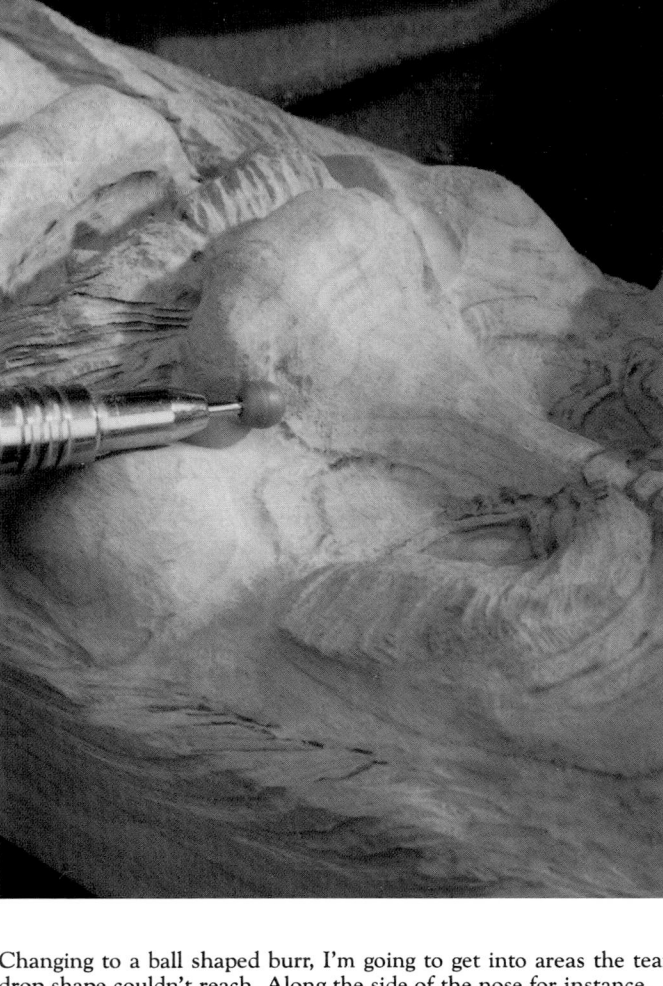

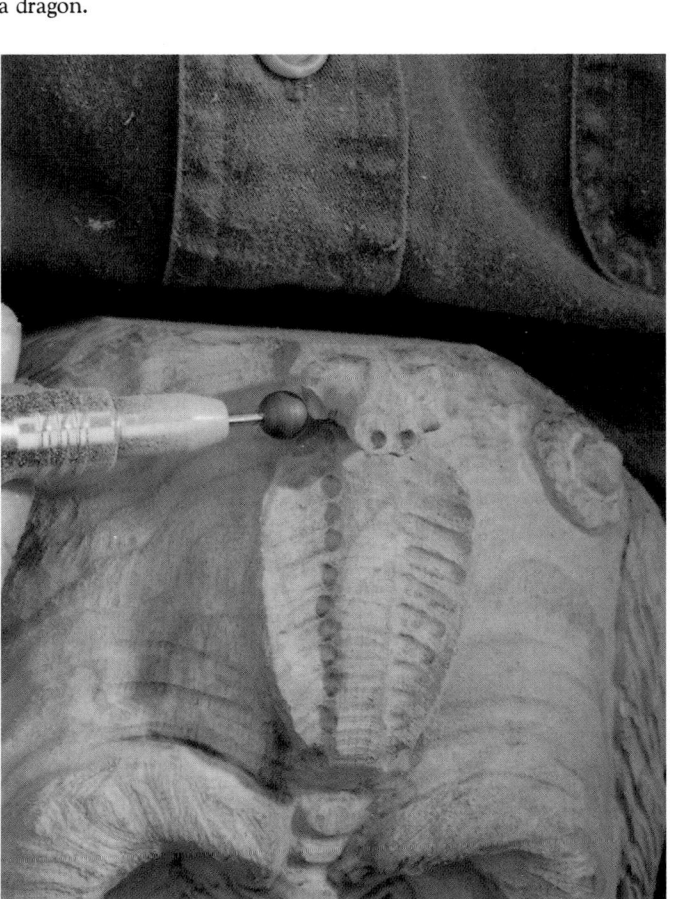

Changing to a ball shaped burr, I'm going to get into areas the tear drop shape couldn't reach. Along the side of the nose for instance.

I'm going to cut down these buggy eyes to give this more of the look of a dragon.

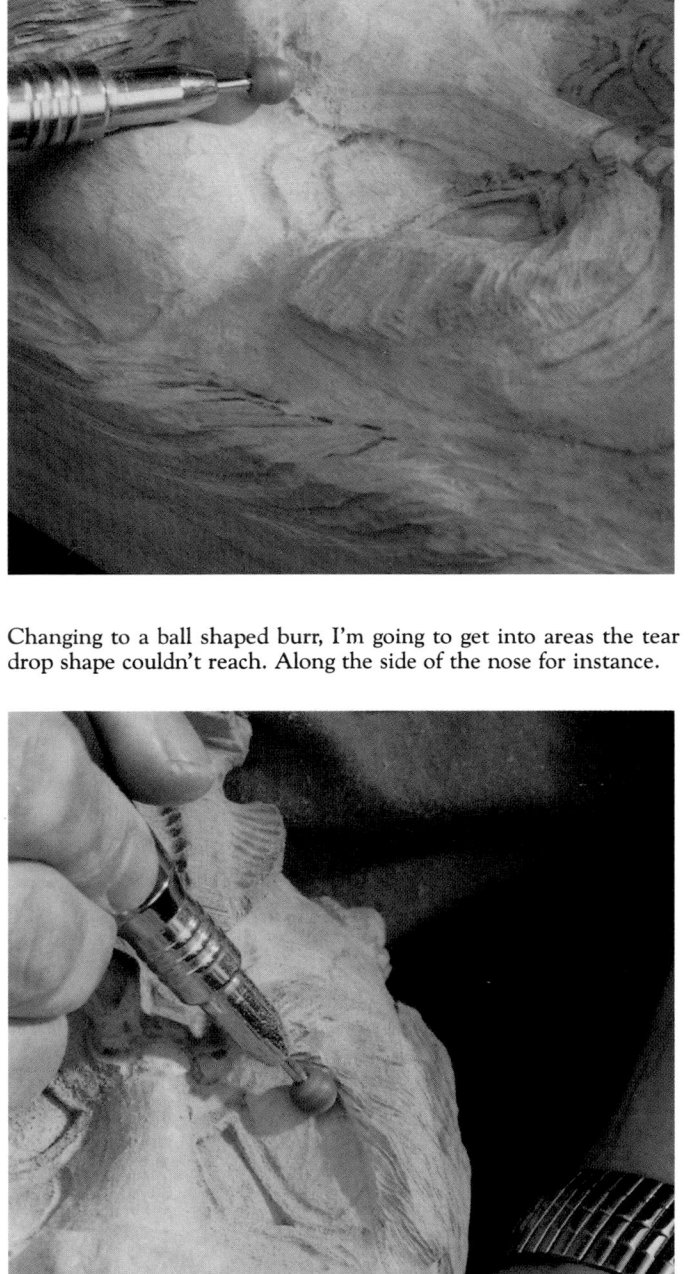

Undercutting the eyelids to create more of a shadow line.

Reducing the eyes.

This little punch makes eyes. It is available through Woodcraft Supply Corp.

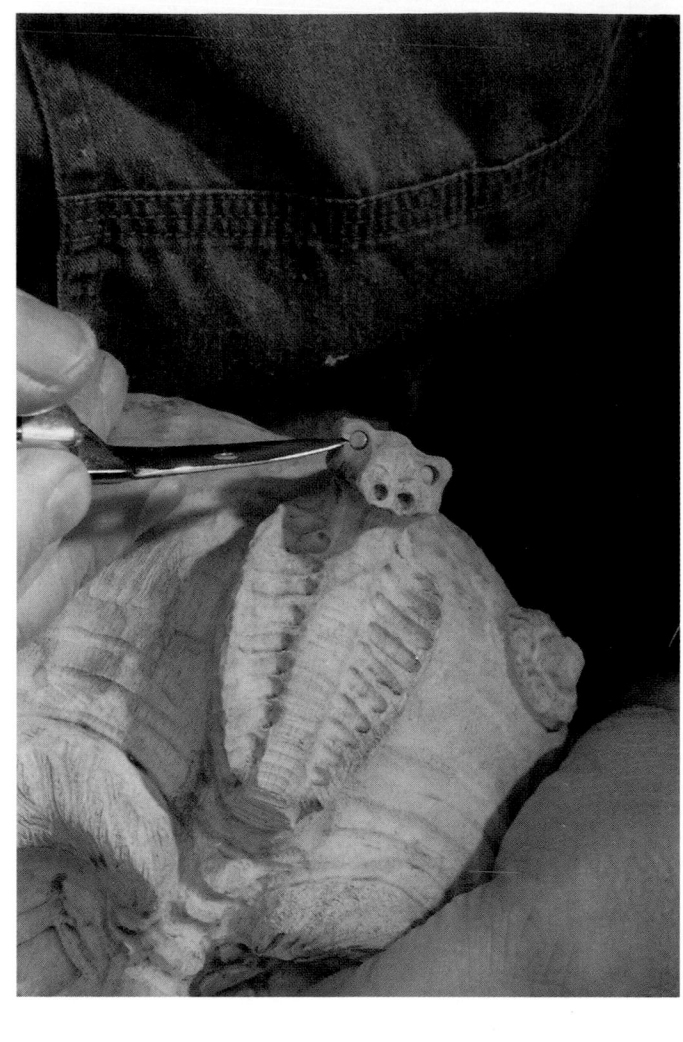

Here are the eyes. Take a little nip from the outer and inner edges of the eyes to give them a little more shape.

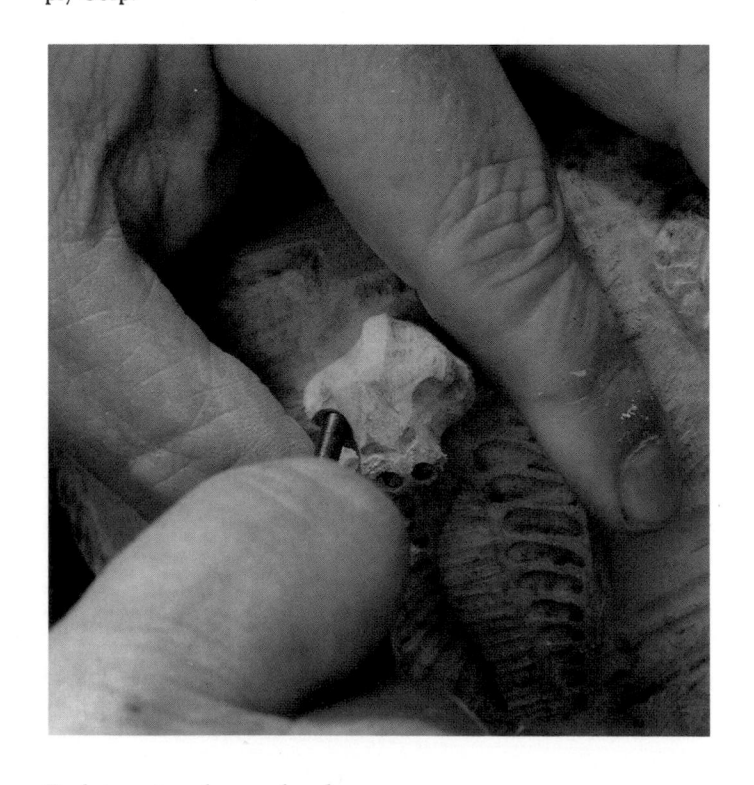

Push it against the wood and rotate.

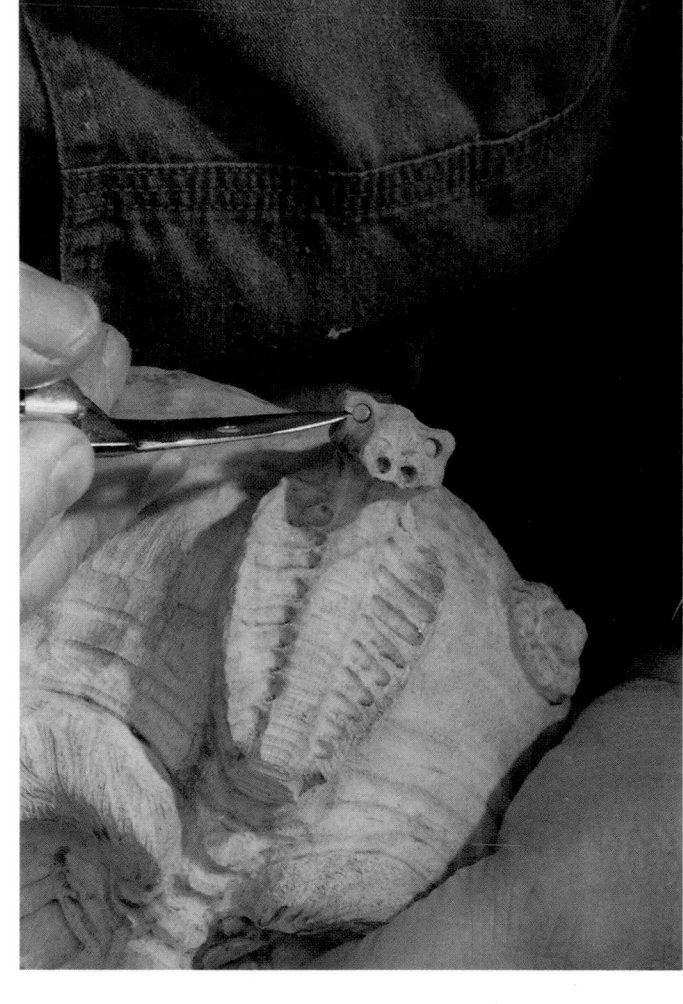

The finished eyes.

Switching to the bigger head with the rougher round burr, I'm going to increase the depth of the mouth back inside. I hope to leave enough of a hollow in the roof of the mouth to carve another set of teeth in the lower jaw.

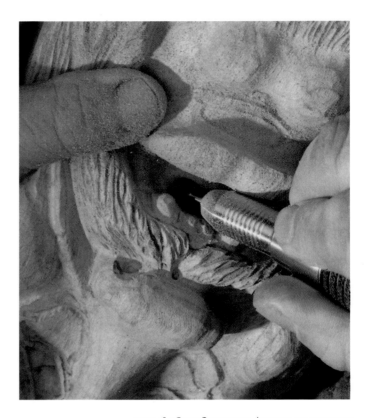

Using the long conical burr, cut straight in along the lines of the teeth.

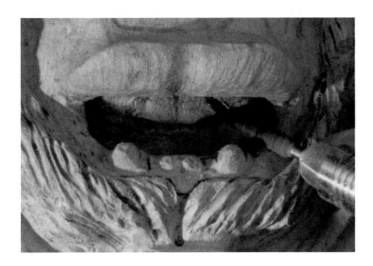

Use a pencil to mark in the lower teeth, or tusks — whichever you like.

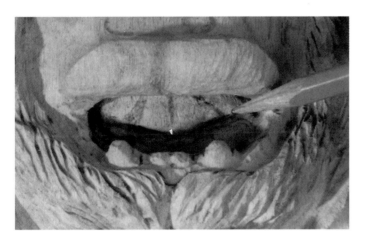

Go all over the work with the High Tech and the larger round burr and smooth out any remaining rough places.

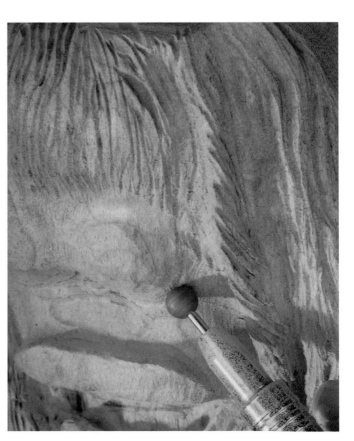

Using a long cone shaped burr in the High Tech, I'm creating the mound of wood that will become the lower teeth. Watch that you don't take the upper teeth out as you put the lower teeth in! This burr is burning the back of the mouth a little but I don't mind. These burn marks deepen the shadows.

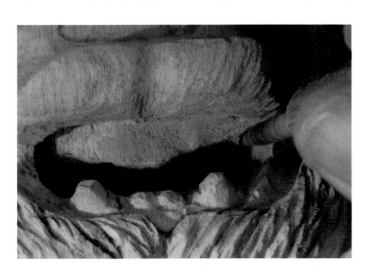

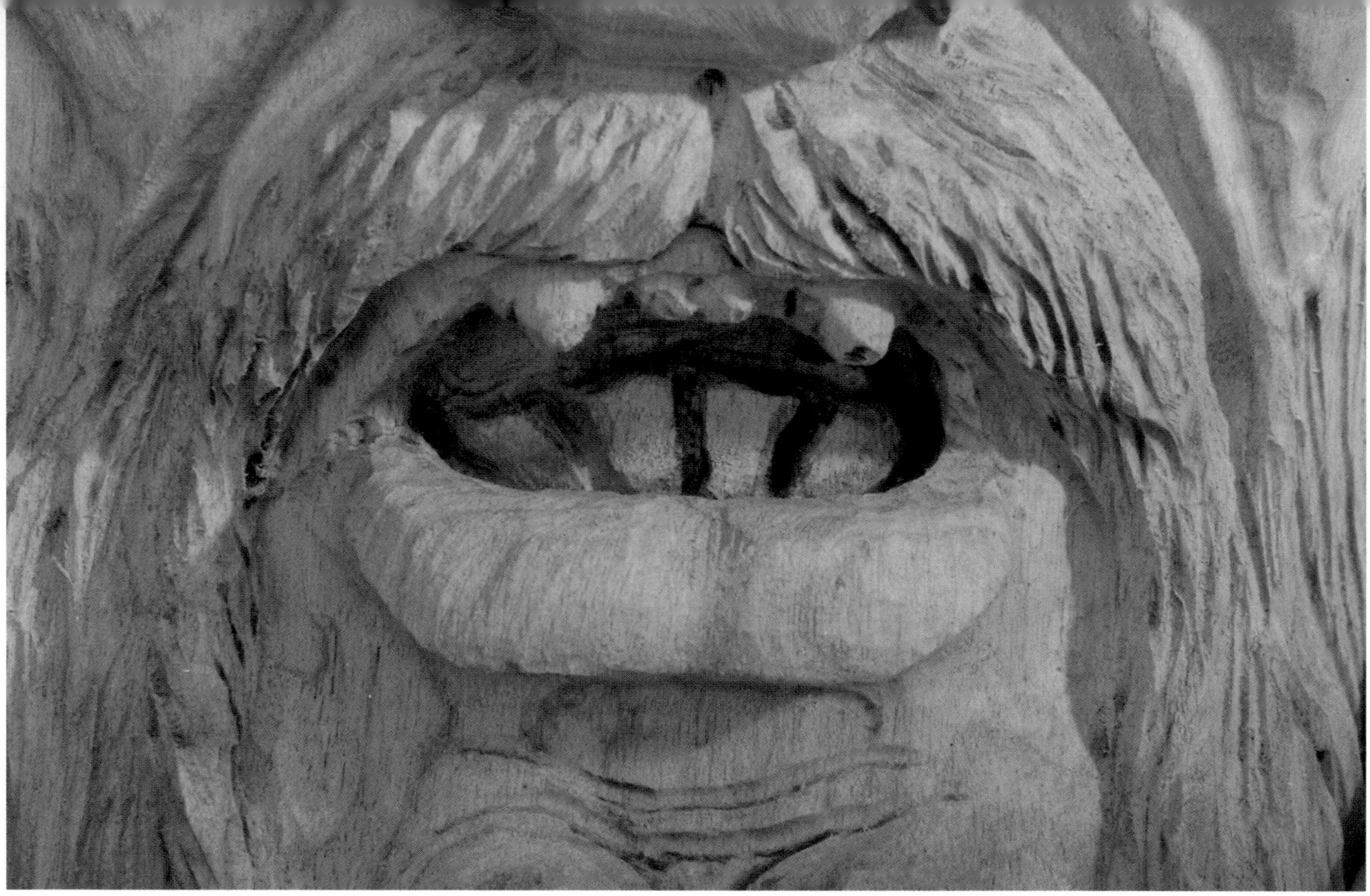

The lower teeth have been cut in.

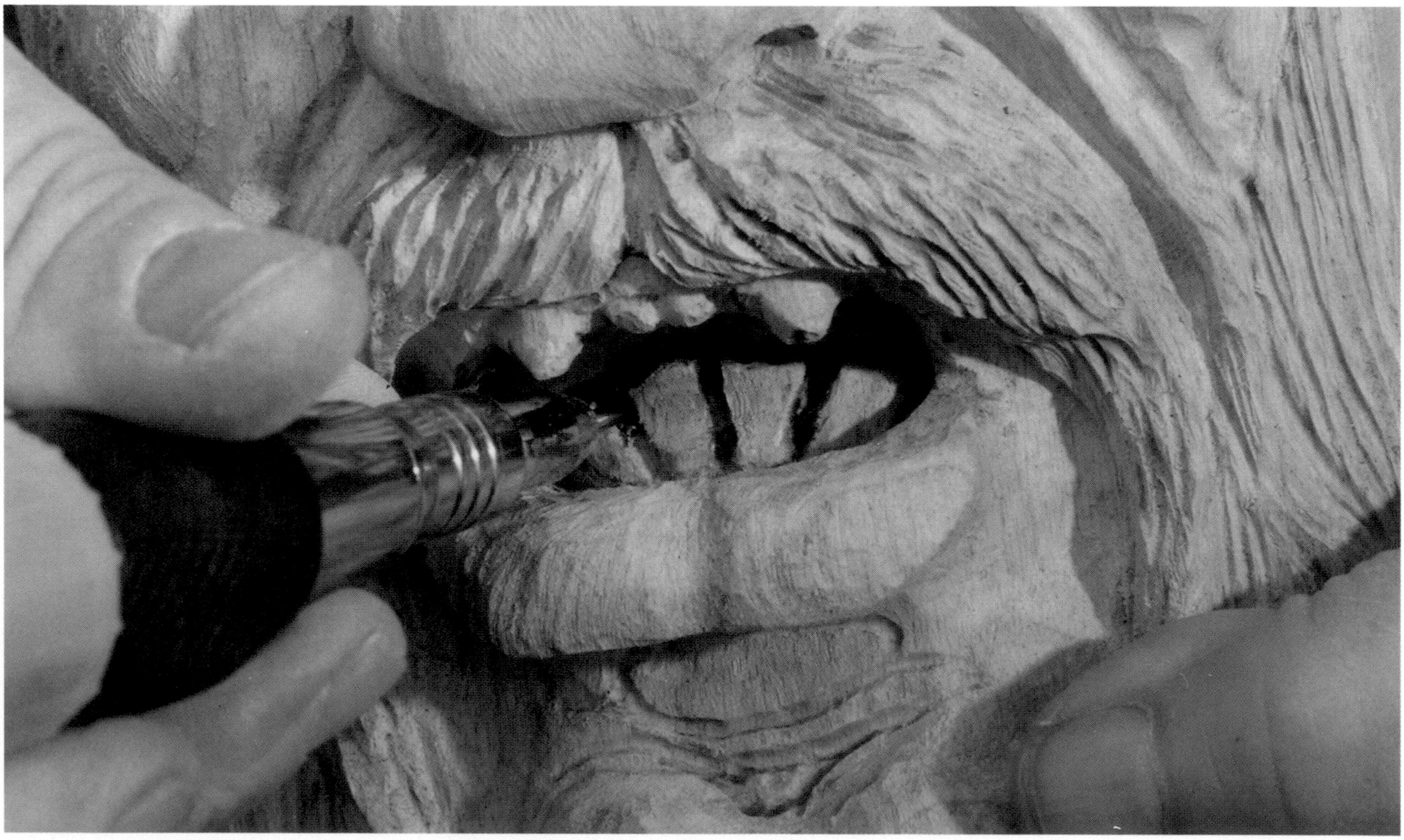

Use the small disk shaped burr to smooth down these lower teeth. This will also reach in behind them, undercutting the teeth and giving them a little depth.

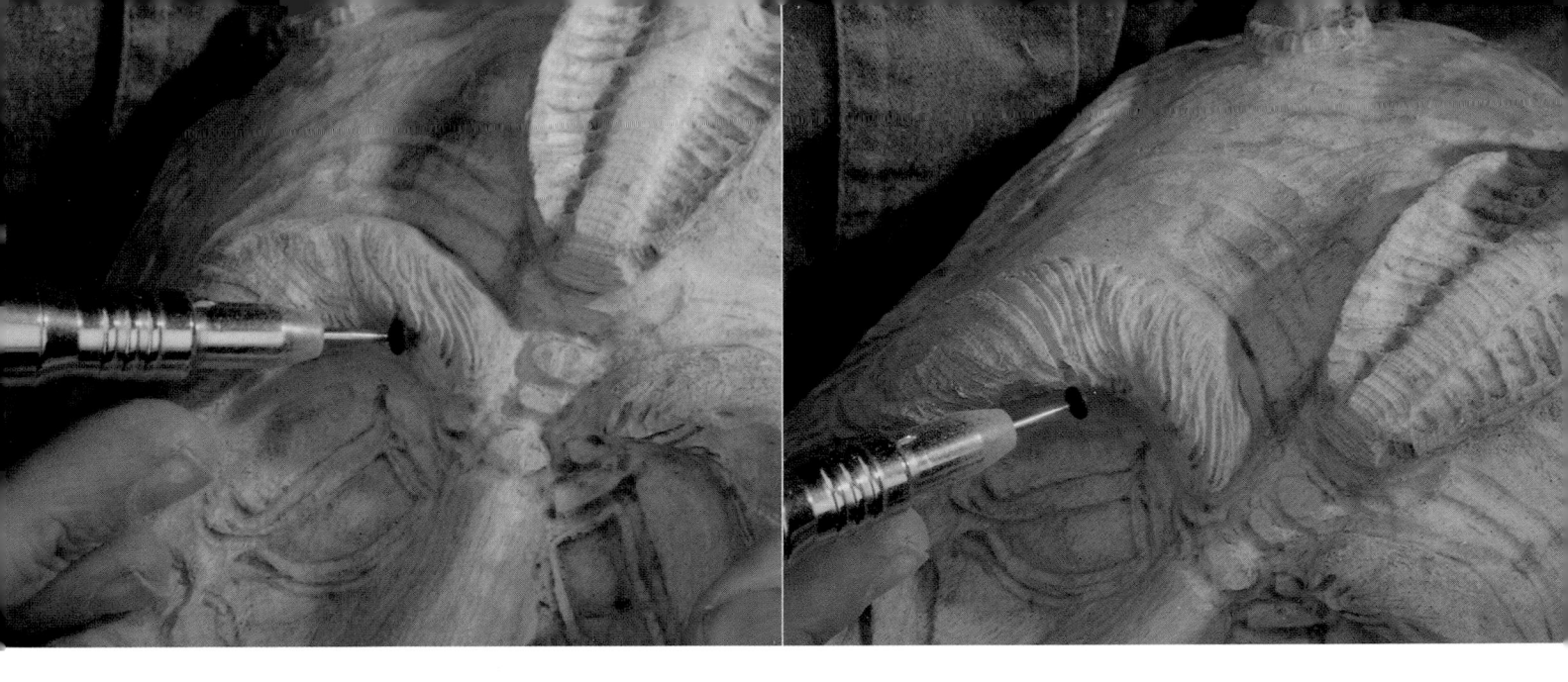

Using the same disk shaped burr, cut in the hair of the eyebrows. Begin in the center using an upward cut and follow the shape of the eyebrow around until you are making almost a downward cut at the lower end of the eyebrows.

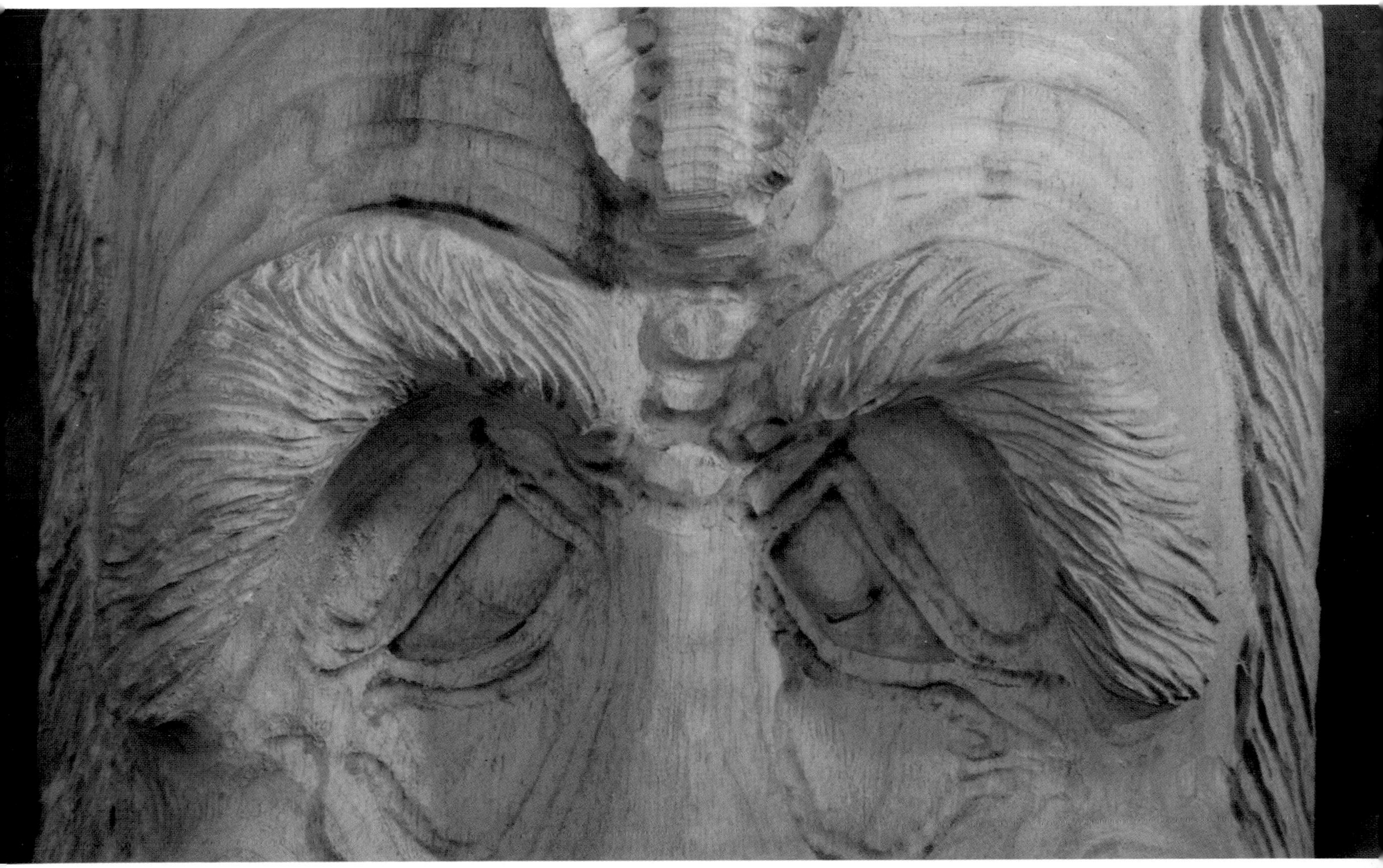

The finished eyebrows.

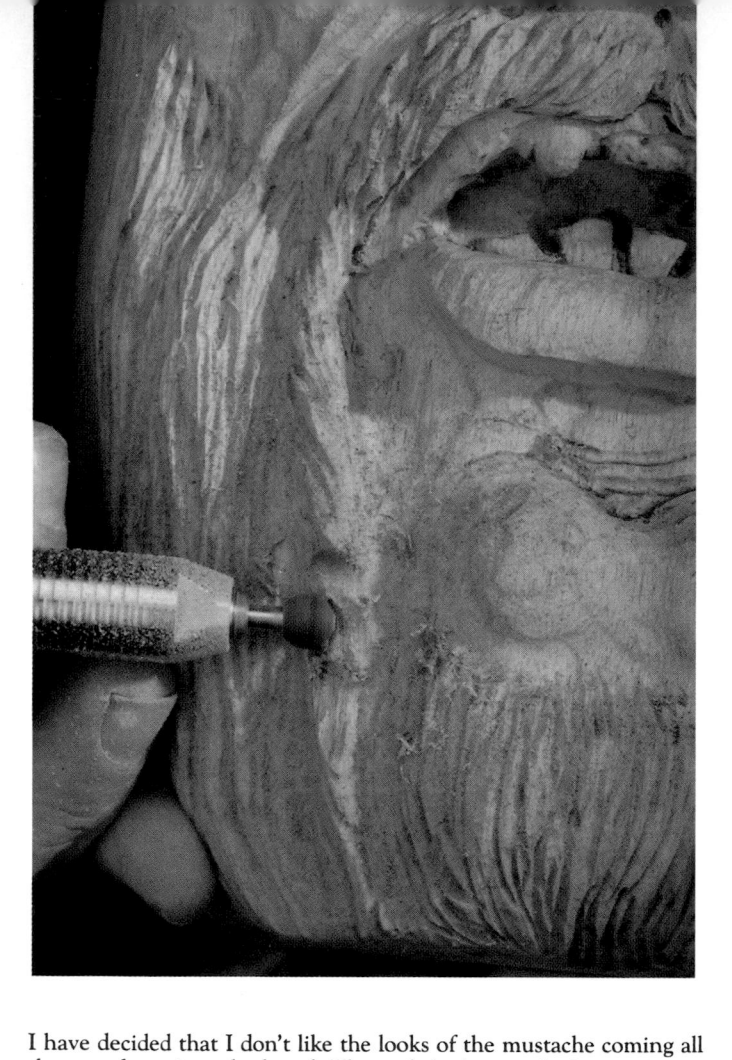

I have decided that I don't like the looks of the mustache coming all the way down into the beard. The ends look scraggly. I am going to shorten the length of the ends using the larger head and a round Kutzall burr. Cutting down the mustache.

Both sides of the mustache have been cut down. Now I need to reestablish the lines of the beard.

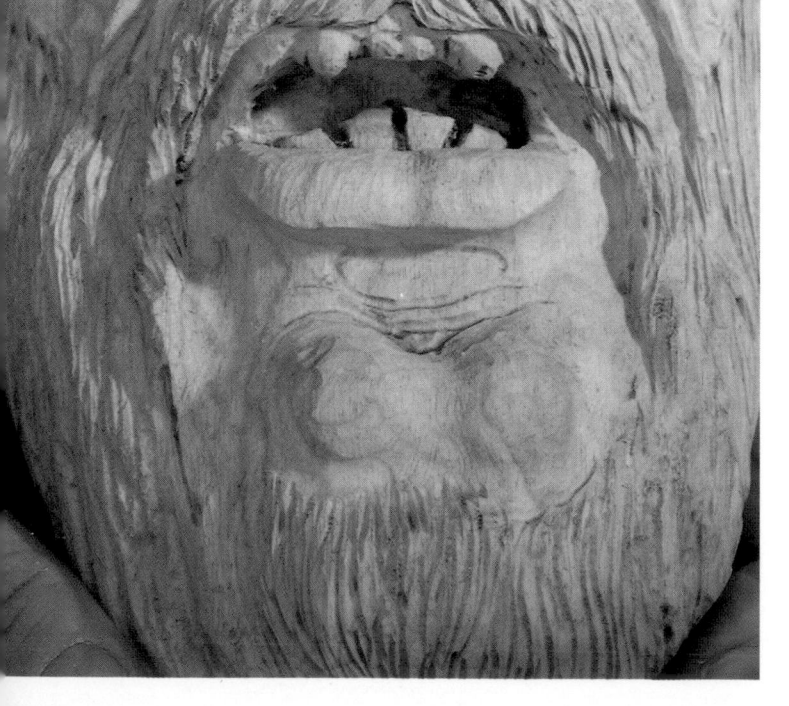

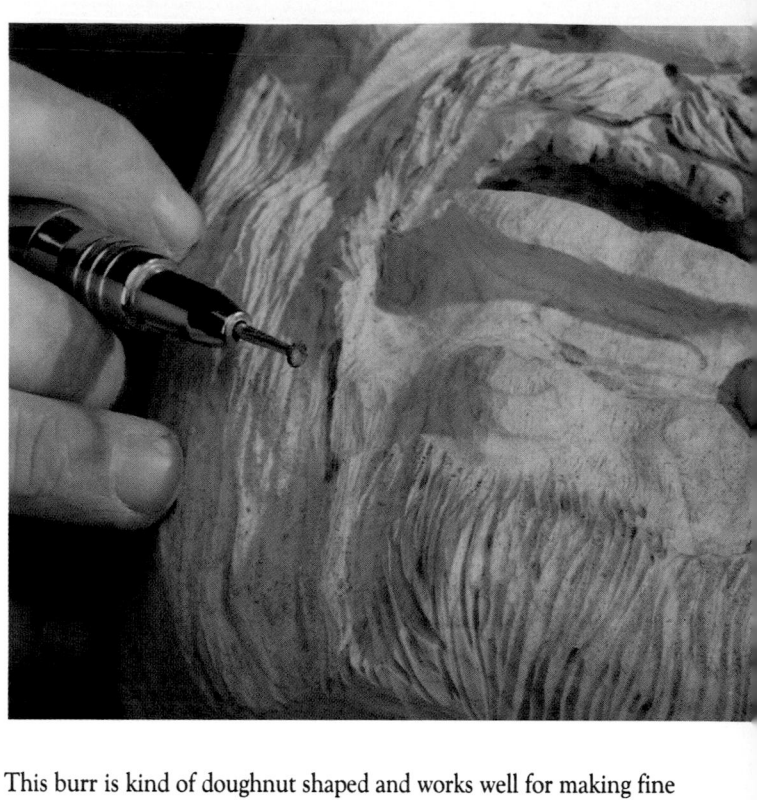

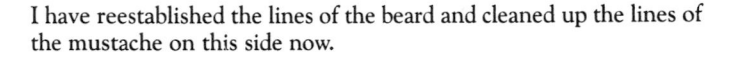

This burr is kind of doughnut shaped and works well for making fine lines in the beard. Experiment with many burrs and see which shapes and sizes work best for you.

I have reestablished the lines of the beard and cleaned up the lines of the mustache on this side now.

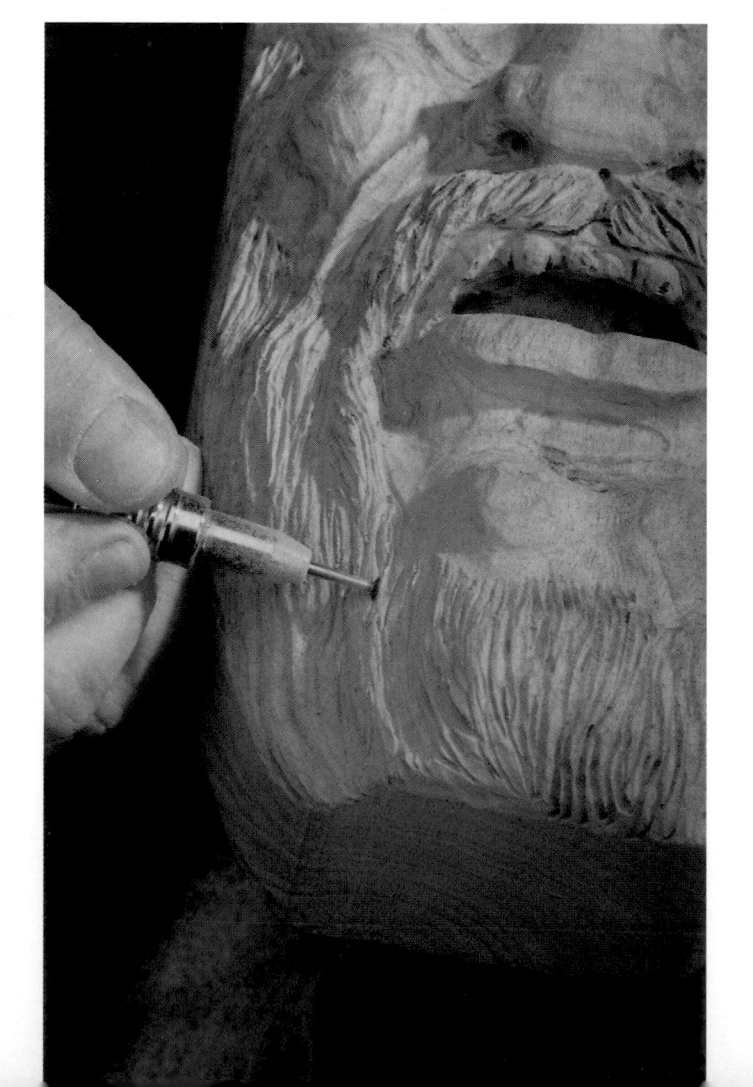

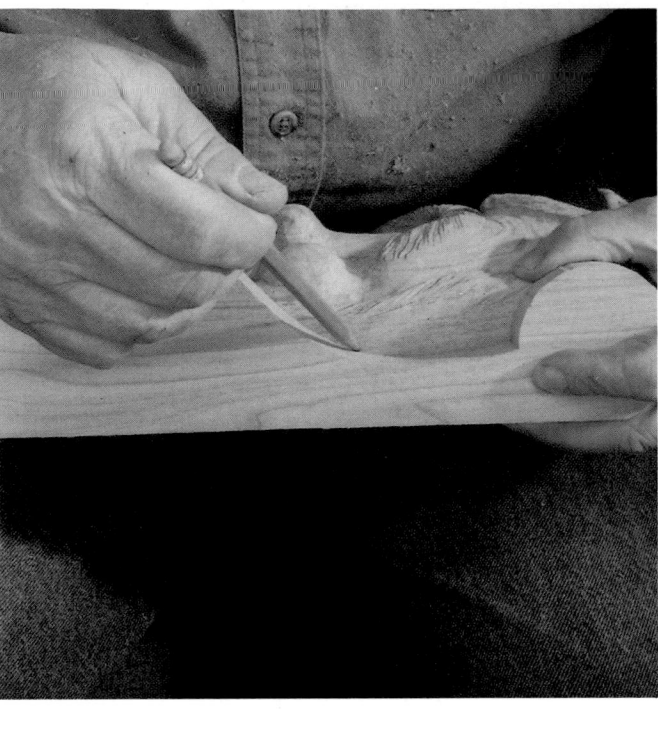

The hair has been added and overlaps the edge of the side panel nicely. There is no undetailed wood visible.

Now it is time to mark in where the side panels meet with the face. Trace the outline of the side panels in pencil on both sides of the face. This will give you guidelines to follow in finishing the details of the hair on the sides of the head.

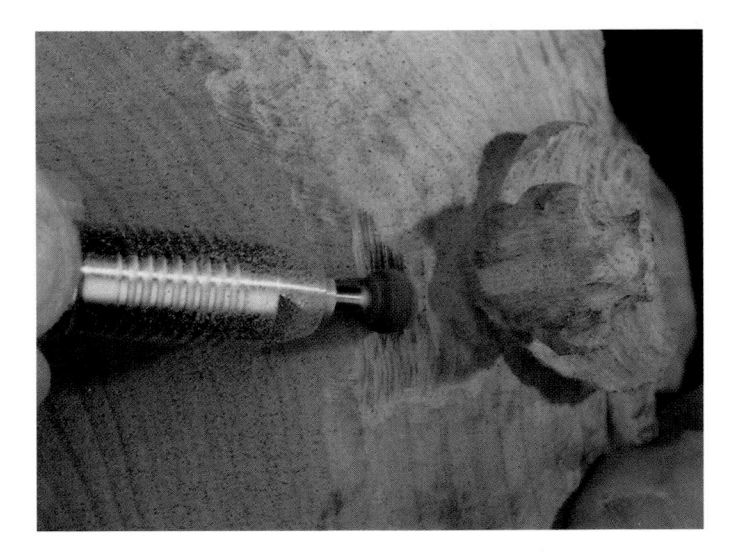

Never forget to go back and look for unfinished places on your piece. There will always be something that needs to be touched up like this small flat spot on top of the house spirit's head.

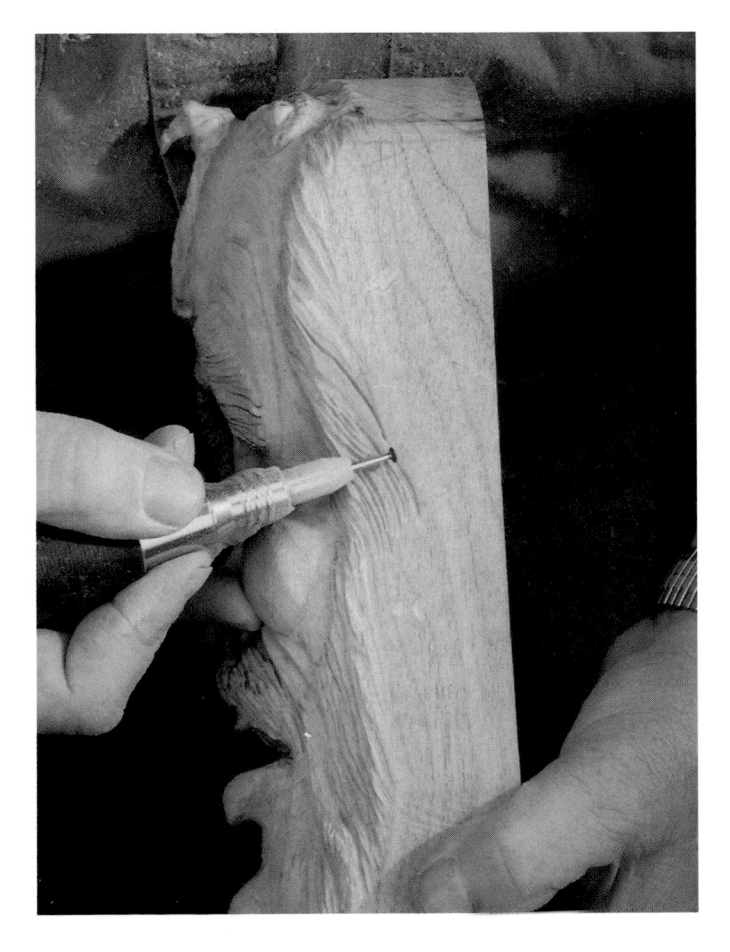

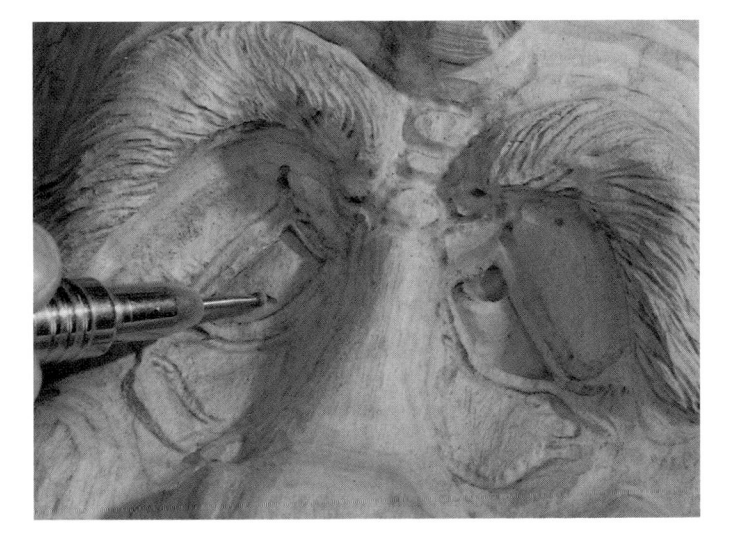

Adding hair to the side of the head down to the pencil guidelines using the same small doughnut shaped burr.

Using a small ball shaped burr in the High Tech, gently place in the iris and hollow out the pupils to finish the eyes.

Using a very small ball shaped burr, I am making sure that the iris' appear to continue on beneath the eyelids rather than stopping or fading out at the edges of them.

The burrs will take the wood down to the finish that 250 grit sandpaper would give you. I'll start sanding down the rough spots this leaves with 300 or 320 grit sandpaper and finish up with 400 grit.

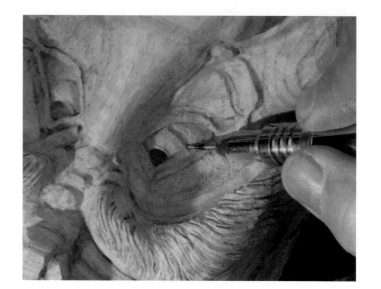

Carve in a small line close to the hollowed out pupil to accentuate it.

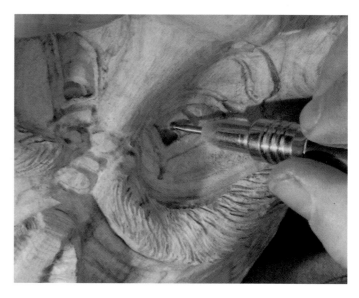

Let your burr undercut the pupil a little to add depth.

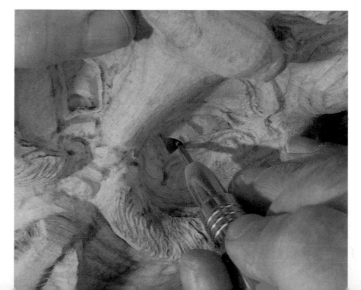

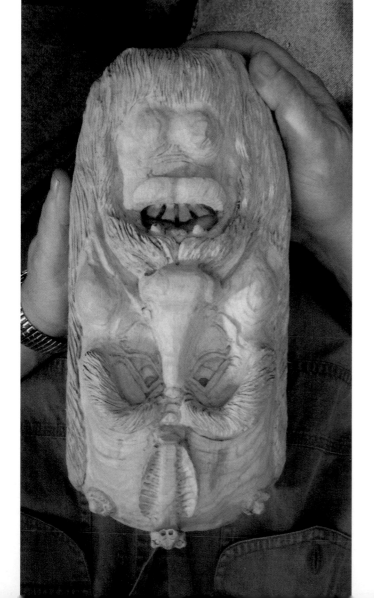

The details are finished on the house spirit.

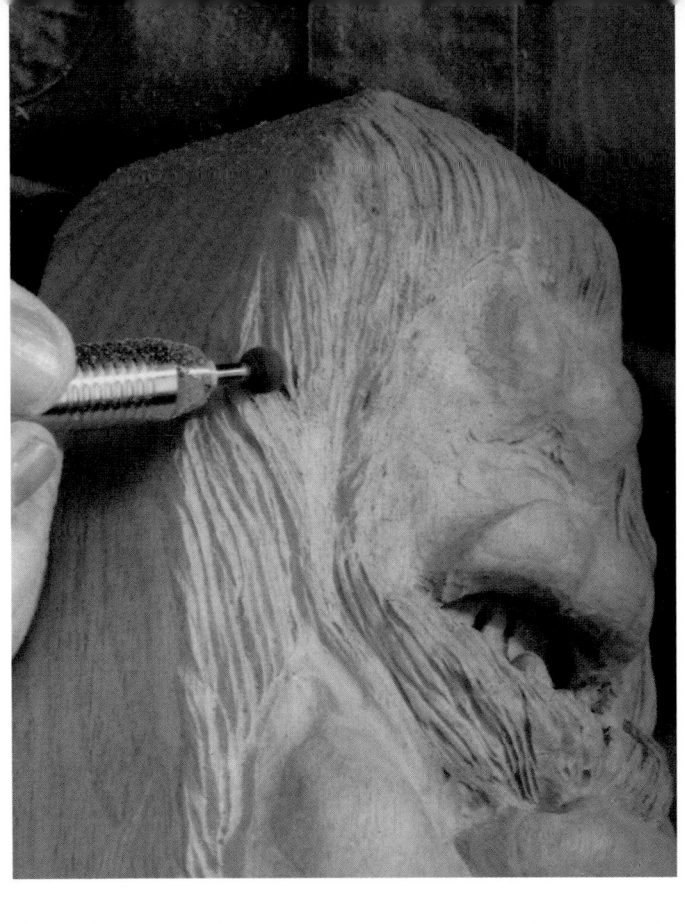

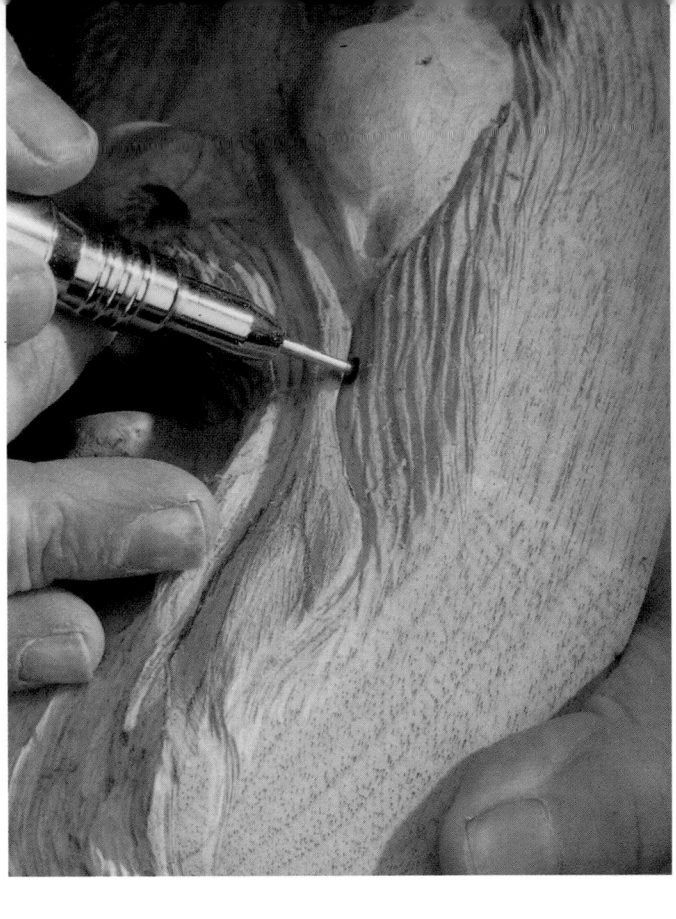

Using a ball shaped burr, smooth out an area in the beard to add a stem and a leaf to give this character a bit more of the feel of a wood spirit. You could just as easily carve in feathers as leaves.

Start outlining along the pencil lines with a disk shaped burr in the High Tech.

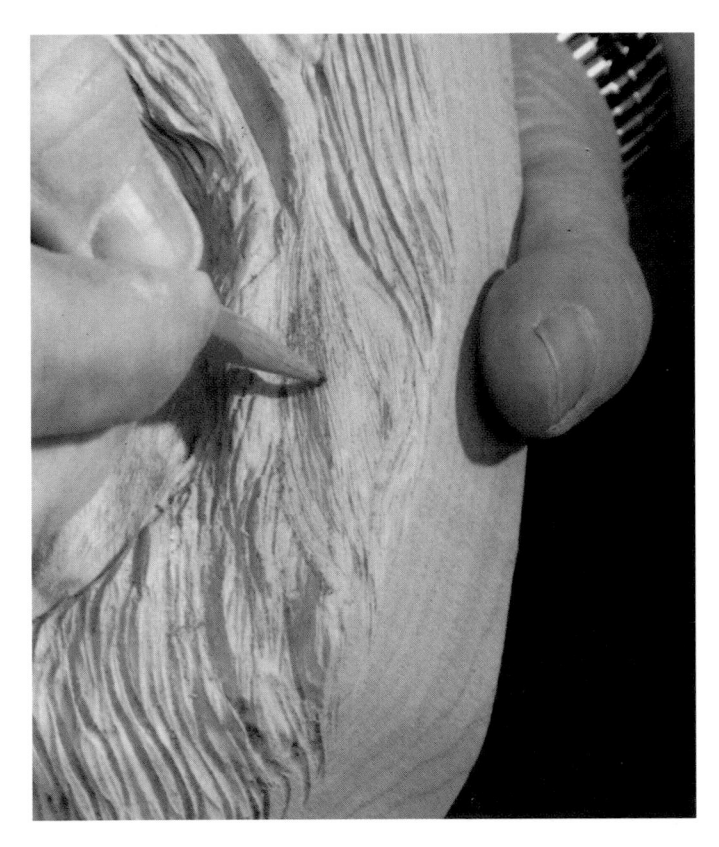

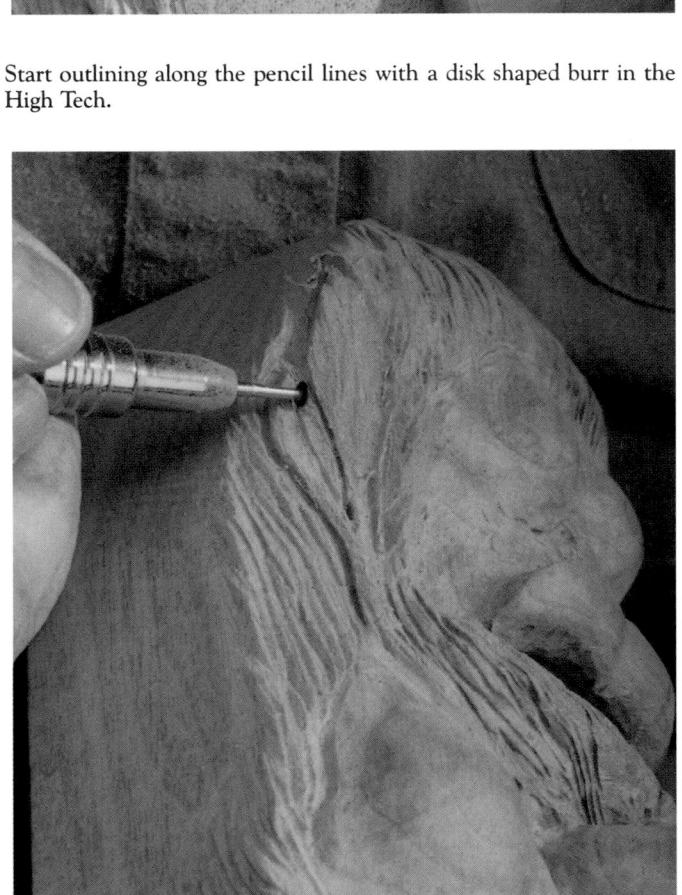

Pencil in the stem and leaf. We'll put two leaves on this side and one on the other. The human eye prefers to see asymmetry in details like this.

Carving in the vein down the center of the leaf.

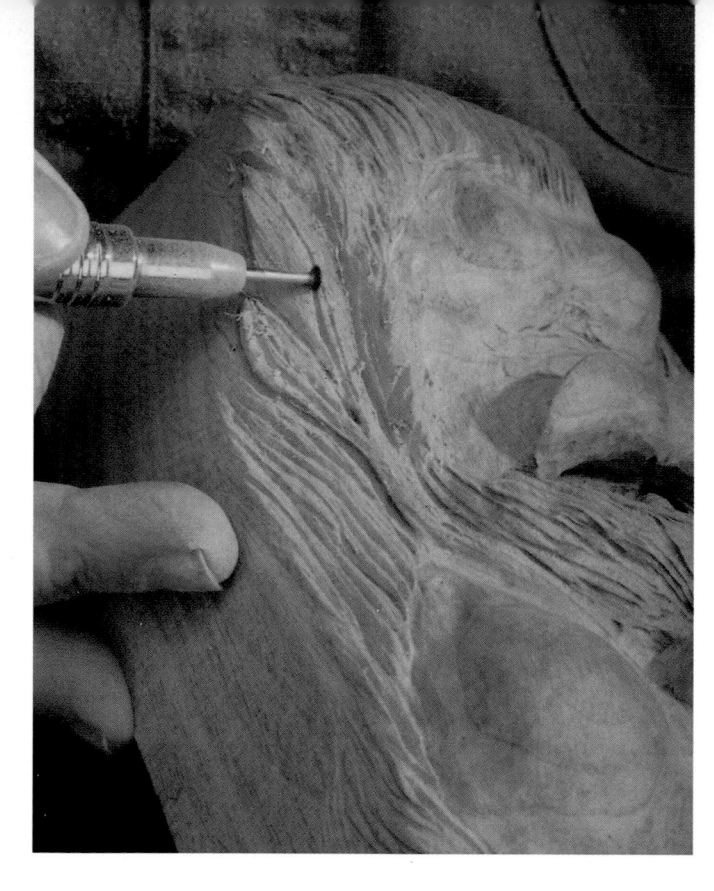

Putting in the central vein on the second leaf and additional details on the first.

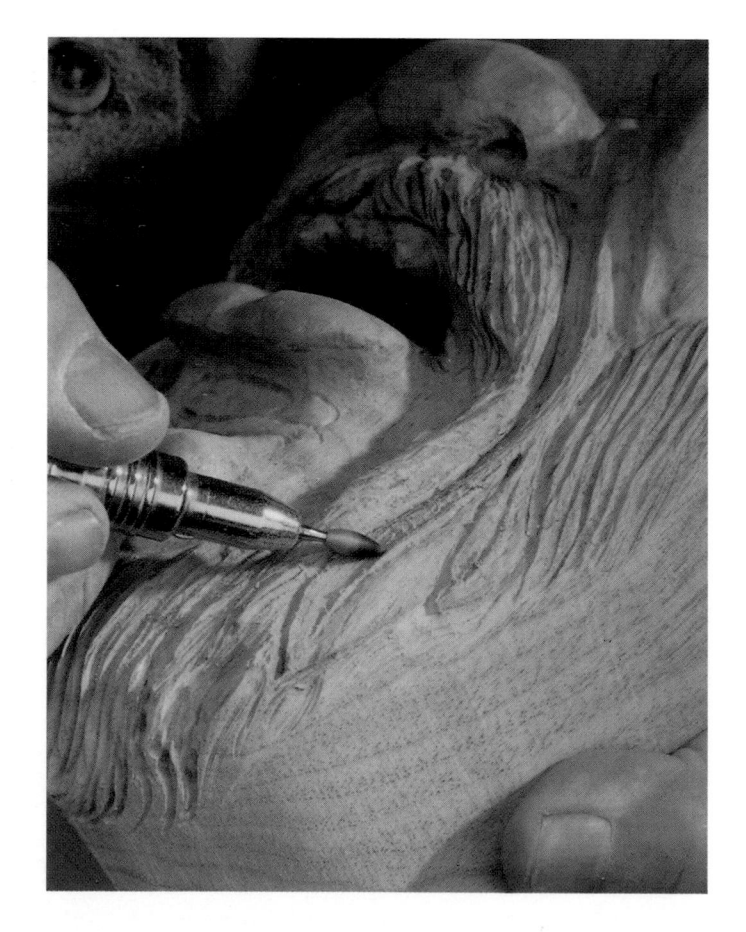

Smooth off the surface of each leaf with a cone shaped burr. Note the raised central vein in the larger leaf.

Use the doughnut shaped burr to add final lines in the hair around the mustache, touching up areas around the added leaves where detail has been removed.

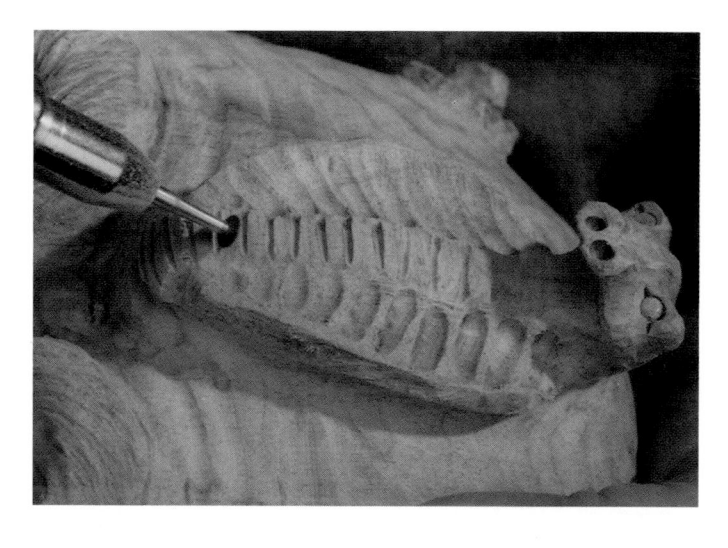

Continue using the small doughnut shaped burr to add scales to the belly of the dragon on the house spirit's forehead.

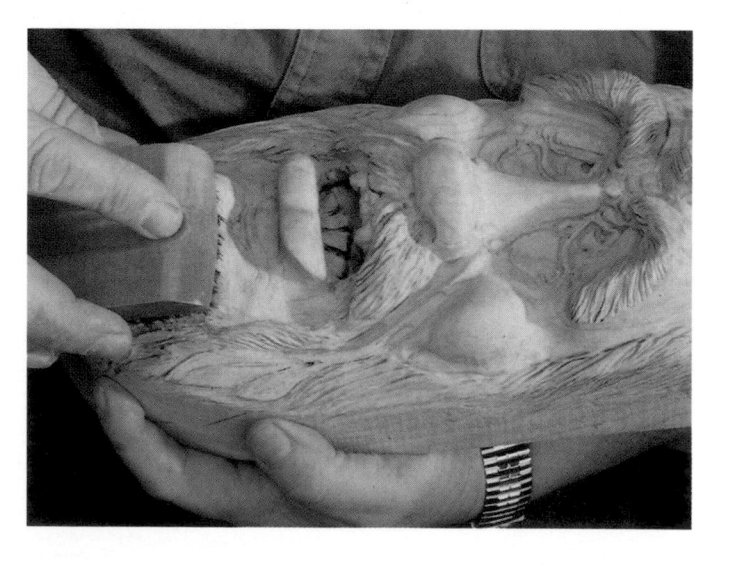

Use a stiff brush to remove the small fuzzies you've missed and to lightly burnish the piece before staining. It will help the figure to hold the stain better.

Don't move your finger from the side of that pencil! Keeping your finger in the same place, mark in lines along the top and outer edge, on both sides of each side panel. Using your finger this way will help you maintain the same distance for the pencil lines along each edge.

Pencil in a cutting line along the side panels. This line will keep the side panel straight on both sides. Use your finger to guide the pencil tip along in a straight line along the length of the wood.

The edges have been carved out.

Using the Ryobi power chisel with a V shaped gouge, follow the pencil lines. I have started at a bad place in the wood that will be hidden along the inside edge beside the wood spirit's head. If I make a mistake starting out here, it won't show! Also, when starting your cut, decide if you want to cut exactly on the pencil line, just inside of that line, or whatever and stick to it throughout to keep your carving consistent.

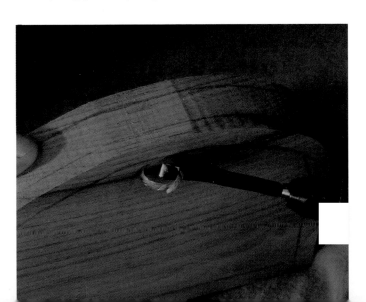

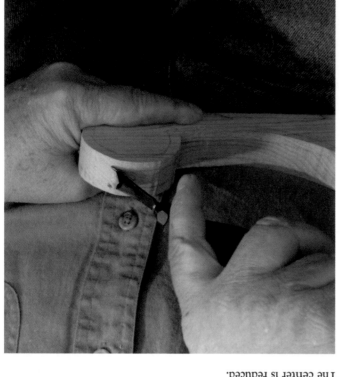

Use a flattened gouge blade and work out from the center of the side panel into the center of the V shaped cut along the edge. This reduces the wood in the center of the side panel to a lower level, leaving a raised outer edge.

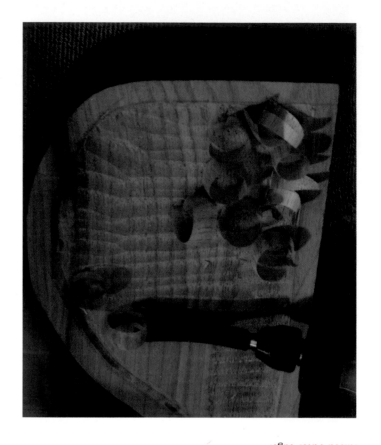

Continuing to reduce the center of the side panel.

The center is reduced.

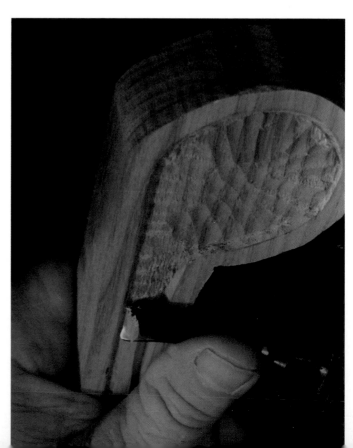

Using a slightly curved gouge, hollow out the center of the edge of the side panel, leaving the outer edges raised here as well. Work downhill and try to keep the center area smooth.

Here is one place that the chisel won't cut straight in, the chisel is too long to get in this tight spot. Cut in sideways in tight spots and come back later with the rotary tool to clean up the cut lines.

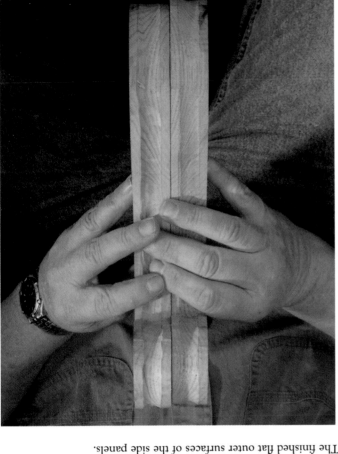

The completed top surfaces of the side panels.

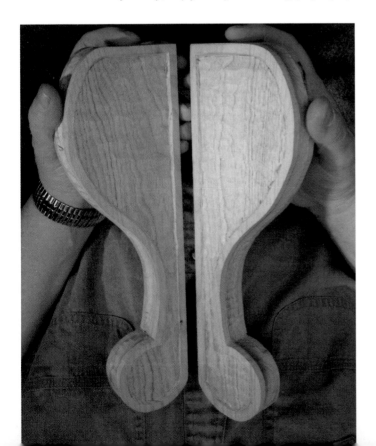

The finished flat outer surfaces of the side panels.

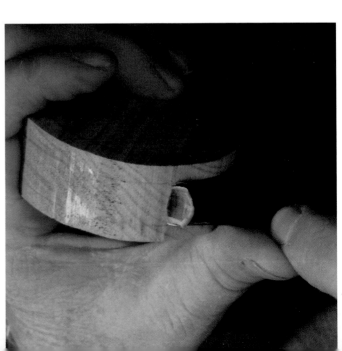

This chisel has a little spring that makes the head with the gouge vibrate. By putting your finger against the flat of the gouge and pulling back on the head, you can control the vibration, giving you better control over your work.

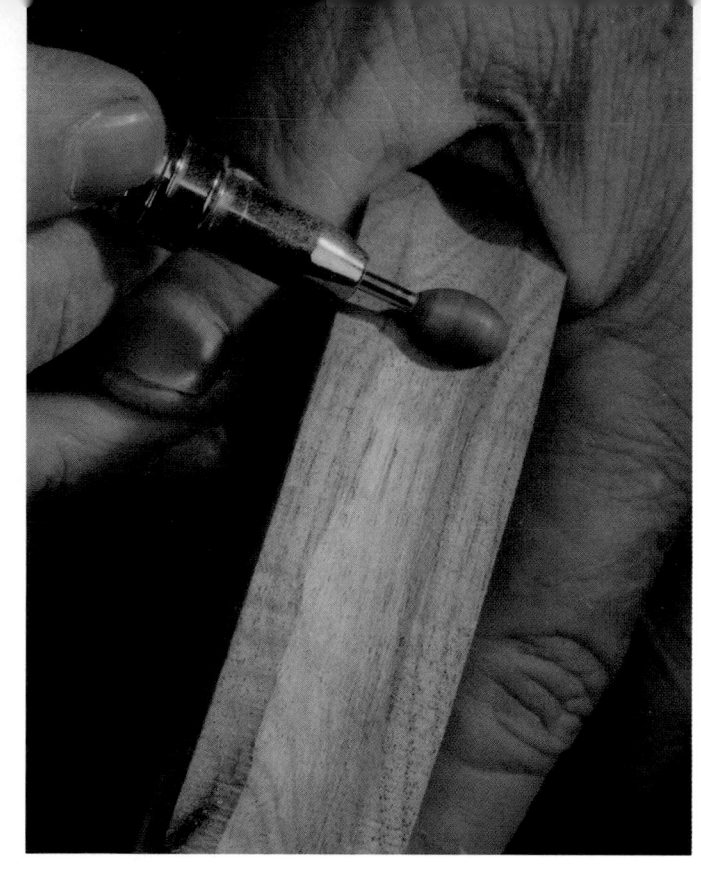

Use a cone shaped burr to smooth down the reduced side surfaces of the panels.

Using the High Tech rotary tool with an egg shaped burr, smooth out the gouged top surface of each side panel.

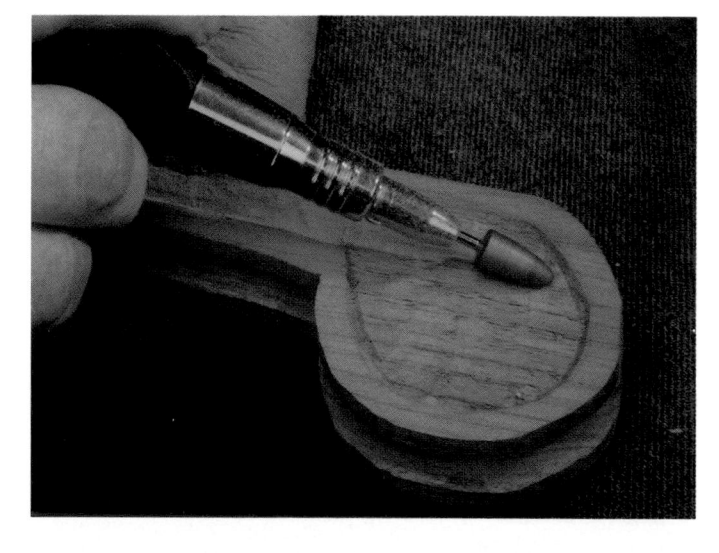

Continuing to smooth.

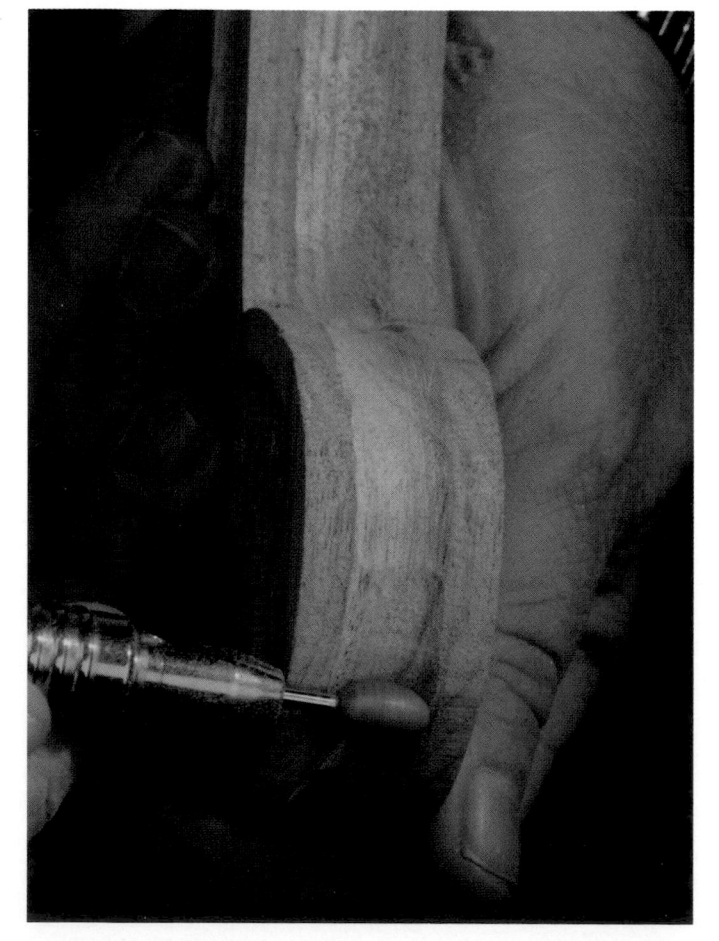

Continuing to smooth.

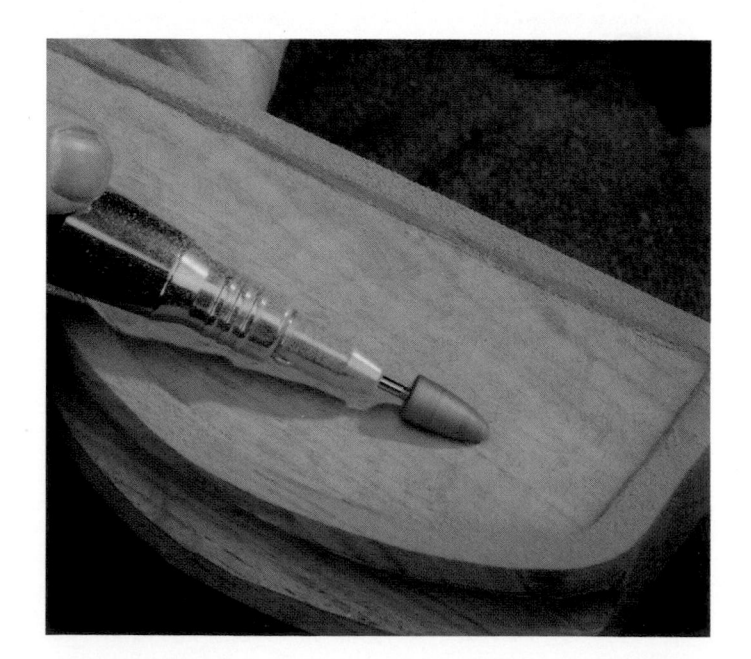

Almost smooth.

The sanded side panels.

Now sand the smoothed surfaces.

We are ready to assemble the parts.

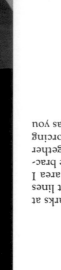

Then I line up the ruler between the marks at either end of the piece and draw straight lines between these four points. This is the area I will route out and into which I will place bracing boards to hold the house spirit together from behind. I do not want the reinforcing wood to show at either end of the piece as you can see from my guide lines.

Lay a strip of wood down along the center lines to make a nice straight center line mark or use a ruler as I am doing here. Using the hole in the end of the ruler to line up on either center mark, I first mark the outside edges on either side of the ruler.

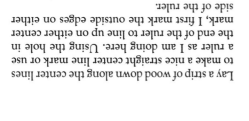

First mark the back of the top and bottom pieces to get the center line.

Using the same technique, mark the center strip down the back of the carved head.

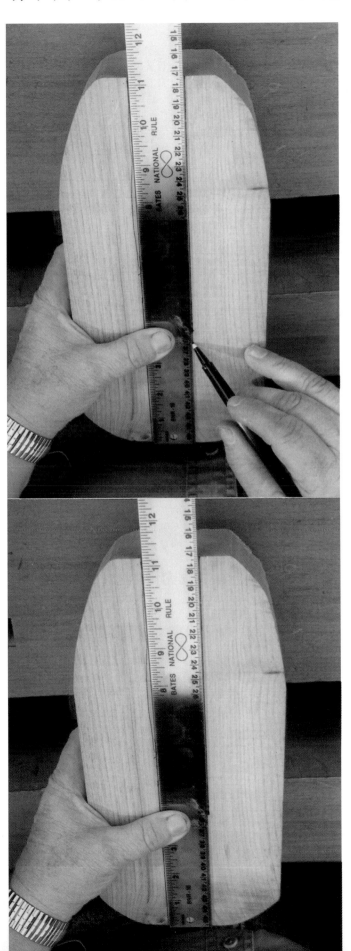

Using the router, begin to cut out the recess into which the back brace will fit. I am starting with the house spirit's head.

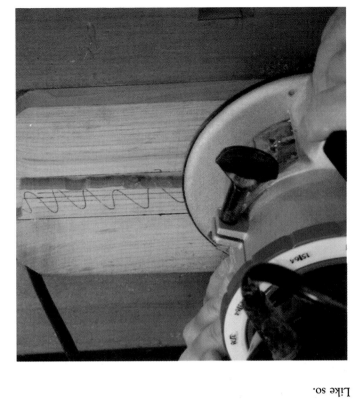

Like so.

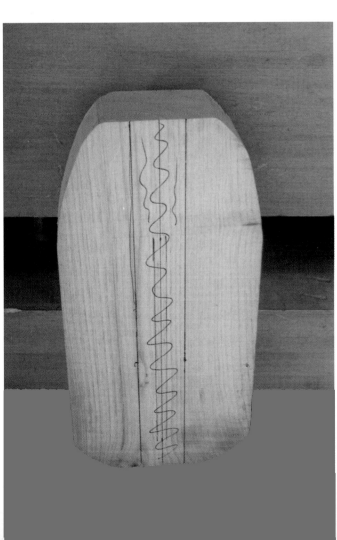

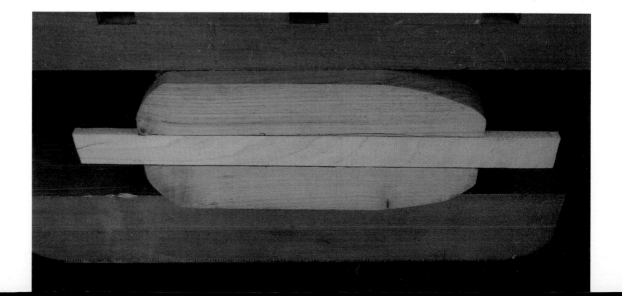

As you finish routing out each piece, check to make sure that the board acting as your back brace will fit into the slot.

Route out the top piece, supporting it tightly in a vice so it won't move.

Again check the fit with your bracing board. Repeat this process on the bottom piece.

Drill pilot holes in the back brace — or braces (in my case I am using two as one was not long enough) — to guide the screw. Place the back brace in place and mark the locations of the screw holes on the rest of the figure.

Like so.

Drill pilot holes in the back of each piece of the house spirit in the marked locations. When working with two pieces of wood bracing, as I am, fasten the screws at both ends first, then mark the middle and fasten the screws.

The back is now braced.

Applying Briwax Golden Oak Stain with a rag. This product is a wax that provides a hard finish. Apply the wax liberally, removing the excess quickly as it dries fast. You can set the waxed pieces aside for a while or just for a few minutes before polishing. Later on down the road you can apply more as you need to. If you need to remove it, turpentine will take Briwax right off.

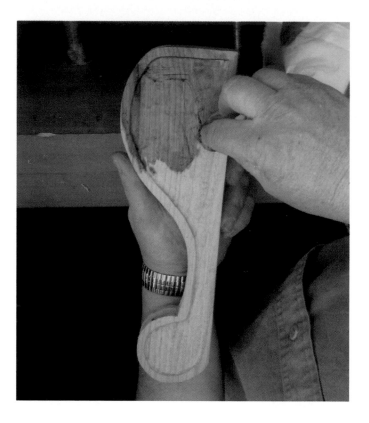

The finished work ready for Briwax Stain.

The finished house spirit.

# Gallery

The completed house spirit project.

House spirit candlestand produced from walnut and mahogany pieces of a pipe organ.

House spirit carved into a lamp of maple and butternut. It is carved with clawed feet.

House spirits carved into large oak timbers salvaged from one of the
oldest hand-hewn houses in the city of Boone, North Carolina.

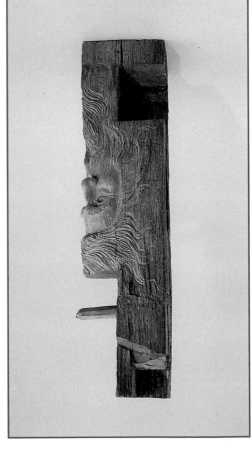

House spirit carved in a plant stand made from two joined mahogany grand piano legs.

House spirits carved into the supports for wall shelves. The gargoyle has a head carved from black walnut and the surrounding body from wormy chestnut. The African face uses walnut across the top and the turnings are of maple and box elder. The small face on the long turned shelf support is a combination of oak, maple and box elder.

House spirit carved into a curly maple rolling pin on a mahogany wall hanger.

House spirit carved in black soapstone, the locals in my neck of the woods call it "black alverine." I have been told that the Indians used this stone for their medicine pipes.